THE LAWYER WITHIN:

Successful Self-Advocacy Techniques

Jeremy T. Robin, Esq.

A&UC Publishing
Boston, Massachusetts

THE LAWYER WITHIN:
Successful Self-Advocacy Techniques
Jeremy T. Robin

A&UC Publishing
Post Office Box 5984
Boston, MA 02114

All rights reserved. No part of this book may be reproduced or transmitted in any form or by any means without the express written consent of the author, except for the inclusion of quotations in a review.

Unattributed quotations are by Jeremy T. Robin

Copyright 2010 by Jeremy T. Robin

ISBN 978-0-9841623-0-7 SAN 858-592X
Printed in the United States of America
Library of Congress Control Number: 2009908317

Robin, Jeremy T.
The Lawyer Within: Successful Self-Advocacy Techniques

*This book is dedicated to
Allison The Great,
Alec The Magnificent,
Hunter The Adorable, and*

To those who are marginalized by our legal system and believe there is no hope. Empower yourselves!

CONTENTS

Acknowledgments	ix-x
Prologue	xi-xv
Warm-Up	xvii-xxii
Part One: Maximizing Negotiation	1-58
A. The Work of a Lawyer in Negotiations	5
B. The Advantages of Effective Negotiation	9
C. Analyzing the Situation	13
D. Your Opponent in Negotiations	14
E. Preparation	17
F. Battle Mentality	20
G. At the Table: Poor Negotiations	21
H. At the Table: The More Effective Way	26
I. When and How to Walk	31
J. Re-Opening Negotiations	34
K. The Broken Deal	37
L. Finalizing the Deal	40
M. Post Deal Niceties	44
N. Dealing with Difficult People – Select Case Studies	47
Part Two: Pursuing Claims & Understanding Rights	59-94
A. Clerical Matters	60
B. Collections	63
C. The Litigation Process in a Nutshell	67
D. Selected Real Estate Matters	69
E. Some Family Law & Probate Cases	74
F. Claims Involving Insurance Companies	79

G.	Everyday Disputes	83
H.	Dealing with the Police	86
I.	A Word on Avoiding Legal Entanglements	91

Part Three: When You Need a Lawyer   95-128
   A. Significant Injury Cases   96
   B. Criminal Cases   100
   C. Family Law Cases   104
   D. Estate Planning   110
   E. Intangible Characteristics of Good Lawyers 114
   F. A Few Words on Judges   126

Final Thoughts   129-130

Appendix   131-172

Afterward   173

ACKNOWLEDGEMENTS

As a shy youth and young adult, I regrettably spent too much time considering others' judgments instead of believing in my abilities. Without the encouragement of certain mentors, my passion for the themes in this book may never have been identified or realized. The first, James Nicholls, was my French professor at Colgate and advisor during my study in Dijon, France. Talk about vivacity! Mr. Nicholls had more enthusiasm and passion in his index finger than many of my colleagues. When he spoke, everything French came alive. Anyone who has one or two teachers like that is blessed. Showmanship and idiosyncrasies aside, Mr. Nicholls' warmth, humor, and playfulness encouraged and instructed me on some of life's most important meanings. Thank you, Monsieur!

Then there was Leonard Salter, my late legal mentor for whom I worked in law school. Leonard, in his eighties when we first met, was as sharp then as any lawyer I have ever encountered. In retrospect, my life, especially my future in the law, didn't make much sense at that time. Confusion was my modus operandi. Leonard made me feel good to be an aspiring lawyer, as his passion and the respect with which he treated others were infectious. Further, he was the author of numerous books on world peace and humanitarianism. What a role model! We became close friends after I opened my office and until his passing in May 2008. I'll forever cherish the final times we met for lunch with his wife Charlotte at his home, discussing politics and the law. How proud he was of me and how indebted I am to his inspiration.

Specific to this project, I am thankful for the work of my two law clerks and scholars-in-training, Jeff Rayball and Jen Reinold. Jen has particularly assisted in the editing and production of this project.

Of course, no acknowledgment could be complete without thanking my beautiful family, beginning with my devoted wife Allison. Your love and understanding are so consistent that I fear taking them for granted. Be assured I appreciate you and everything you mean to us.

Alec and Hunter, my two boys, surely do not comprehend how a coy smile or an act of affection makes their daddy feel. One day they will.

PROLOGUE

This is my second adventure in the world of nonfiction legal writing. I wrote my first book, *Unlearning Law School: The Key to Running Your Own Office* to inspire law students and dissatisfied lawyers to open their own offices. As the title suggests, that spiritual project provided an approach for the successful solo practice of law. The supportive response of students, lawyers, law schools, and book sellers has humbled me.

Unlearning Law School may seem incompatible with the current project. If *The Lawyer Within* succeeds in any fashion, I will have empowered at least one person to represent himself with effectiveness or to secure the proper lawyer if the case requires representation. My attorney colleagues may scoff at this effort, as some already have, and it may appear to be financially foolish. I am, after all, in the law business, which means that I want to obtain, and not discourage, potential clients.

But my office is thriving. Our society, unfortunately, is not as healthy. Consumers, in particular, are often derailed by corporate and administrative forces in this country. When they have a legal issue, they rush off to call a lawyer and waste hundreds to thousands of dollars doing so. I'm not saying they always receive bad representation, only that it may be un-

THE LAWYER WITHIN

necessary. Alternatively, those faced with a legal issue may attempt to handle it on their own, but fail to do so in an effective manner.

Let's return to my objective in writing this book. The idealism bug has either energized or afflicted me, depending on your perspective. Making the legal system more available to those, in my view, who need it the most (namely consumers and individuals like you and me) drives me.

As I write, it is 2009. Though statistics, accounts, and surveys vary, something like 1% of the American population owns 40% of the country's wealth. That's astounding. When it comes to the law, our system supports the wealthy, insofar as they can afford competent attorneys to navigate through the maze of obscure and confusing legal rules, precedent, and procedure. Our system also helps indigent litigants, who are afforded free attorneys in certain cases. For the most part, though, you're on your own if you can't afford to spend the tens of thousands of dollars it may cost to pursue or defend litigation proceedings. Knowledge and self-confidence are great equalizers.

I'm getting a bit sidetracked here, so let me try to connect the dots. If our culture and current government are so anti-progressive when it comes to protecting the proverbial little man, you've got to do it on your own.

In a nutshell, that's what *The Lawyer Within* addresses.

To the extent I can succeed in arming non-lawyers to advocate effectively for themselves, in an ironic way, I believe I can actually grow my law business and those of other attorneys. How? Self-advocacy and independence breed happiness, and I have to believe that having happier people in a society benefits the wealth of community members-including small business owners. With more money around, people have increased spending power and will in turn hire lawyers for jobs which require representation. *The Lawyer Within* does not stand for the proposition that non-lawyers can and should represent themselves in all instances. Far from it. What I'm saying is that

PROLOGUE

there are many situations when a non-lawyer can do so to build self-esteem and save the aforementioned legal costs.

I've broken *The Lawyer Within* into three parts. Part One deals exclusively with negotiation. Contrary to popular belief, I believe that effective lawyering requires exceptional negotiating skills. The media era has exaggerated the importance of trial lawyers, as all of the cases we seem to read about and watch on television focus on multi-million dollar judgments. When was the last time you read about the successful negotiation of a boundary dispute between two neighbors? In reality, that's the type of dispute which affects our lives on a more regular basis.

In Part Two, we discuss cases and claims which a non-lawyer can handle on his own. From a numbers standpoint, this covers most matters. Though a non-lawyer has the ability to represent himself in these cases, failing to implement the proper strategy or use the best techniques may obstruct success. That's not to say that one needs to spend hours studying a manual on how to act as his own lawyer. I'll concede that you should investigate the protocol of the court, agency, or other forum in which you are advocating. But, here's the kicker: Representing yourself is not as tough as it may seem. I'm reminded of the immortal words of our thirty-second President, Franklin D. Roosevelt: "...the only thing we have to fear...is fear itself." Most of us have sufficient common sense to navigate through the minutiae of legal proceedings and to resolve everyday issues. It is fear and perhaps ignorance of the legal process which inhibit us. The oftentimes arrogant and demeaning nature of lawyers doesn't help. Further, those who believe you need an Ivy League degree or some impressive pedigree are mistaken. In my experience, lawyers with such eye-catching resumes often fail in representing the interests of their clients, They're too consumed with their own distorted sense of importance.

Part Three identifies cases in which one would be well-served to hire a lawyer. Once you've isolated these matters which, as indicated, represent a small percentage of the total, there are certain other issues to consider concerning whom you should hire. Make sure you interview enough candidates until you find one with whom you feel comfortable. Research your prospect to determine if he or she has the right qualifications and do not hesitate to ask appropriate questions concerning strategy and the subject matter. Finally, investigate what comparable lawyers charge for similar services to eliminate overcharging. We talk in this section about assessing candidates on the basis of their responses to your specific questions. Merely because you must hire a lawyer should not mean you blindly and passively grant him or her unbridled authority.

    Having spoken a bit about my objective in writing *The Lawyer Within* and summarized the contents, I'd like to conclude these introductory remarks by sharing with you what motivates me to write a book such as this. I don't want to repeat the entirety of what I wrote in *Unlearning Law School*, though its essence is applicable here. In *Unlearning Law School*, I proclaimed that my happiness expands when I can share with others.

    What has inspired me to an even greater degree with *The Lawyer Within* is that I now have a larger audience. Though *Unlearning Law School* addressed topics which are applicable to businesses in general, it targets the law business. One million lawyers practice in the United States, a large number. Our country's population, however, is roughly four hundred sixty million. One in four hundred sixty is a small percentage.

    Conversely, *The Lawyer Within* promises a more diverse readership. We all encounter legal issues at some point and can benefit from an effective strategy. Whether you are a life insurance salesman, a teacher, an auto mechanic, an investment banker, a sales associate, a financial specialist, etc, the chances are good you will frequently be in a position to help yourself by implementing effective self-advocacy concepts. In other words, with *The Lawyer Within* I'm able to positively affect more people. That's both exciting and humbling.

    In my view, the thrill of empowerment has no peers. There's

… no amount of money, status or notoriety which brings me that degree of satisfaction. I think it's the major building block of self-esteem. The opposite, unfortunately, holds equal truth: Self-victimization leaves one feeling distraught (at best) or depressed (at worst). The good news is that opportunities for self-representation, as we'll discuss, are plentiful. By taking the initiative, I submit you will grow your self-esteem—in addition to your pocketbook.

The notion of easing and perhaps bettering the lives of people whom I've never met gives me a feeling of satisfaction which makes this project worthwhile regardless of its material success.

WARM-UP

Let me level with you. I'm a bit torn as I begin to write. On the one hand, I feel it's important to fill *The Lawyer Within* with nuggets of coarse legal advice and information such that it can become a reference book of sorts. For example, if someone were contemplating the eviction of a tenant, he or she could flip to the appropriate chapter and page which addresses that process.

On the other hand, spirituality gets lost if I'm too organized in this fashion, as do humor and a large margin of my target audience. Further, there are an abundance of legal handbooks which are far more comprehensive than this one and which were written by lawyers far older than I. More to the point, I'm more comfortable when I write as I would speak.

Everyone knows an athlete performs his or her best after an adequate warm-up and perhaps a motivational or relaxation technique. To my knowledge, this approach has rarely, if ever, been implemented in a book. That's my challenge.

People are different in so many ways, from appearance to sense of humor to interests, etc. In addition to requiring certain necessities (e.g. food and water), we all need love—to give it and receive it. What does this have to do with anything? Well, I've noticed that giving and receiving love are conditioned on feeling good about yourself. That good internal feeling grows when we feel confident. Confidence in turn comes from seeing ourselves stand up to challenges and rally for ourselves when circumstances and/or people conspire to bring us down.

Here's a shocker: Life is tough. People who have achieved great things have overcome the force of those who sought to derail them. I'm reminded of Einstein's words: "Great spirits have often encountered violent opposition from weak minds." Let's look at history. Think of Jackie Robinson. Modern America lauds his accomplishment in breaking the race barrier in professional baseball, and his uniform number has been retired by every team in his honor. But consider what it was like for him in the 1950s when he was playing baseball in segregated America. He received death threats for upsetting the white make-up of the league. People spit and threw things at him. Opposing players and teammates, in large measure, were resentful. Each time he stepped to the plate, took the field, or rode in the team bus he was heckled and verbally abused. Can you imagine that kind of pressure? I can't. Yet he performed at an all-star level on the field and kept his composure. It gives me some perspective in terms of my minor complaints in life.

What about folks like Einstein and Edison? Think their successes were purely the products of natural ability? Wrong. To paraphrase Edison: "Success is 90% perspiration." Of course, their sharp, creative minds were at play. But we are all geniuses at something(s). My wife, for example, is visually creative. I'm astounded at how easily she can size up a room with respect to furniture, window treatment, and color coordination needs. When she's done, a shabby area is transformed into one of palatial proportions. Of course, managing the budget is another issue!

The key to discovering our individual geniuses, I believe, is developing the self-confidence necessary to take on the forces of apathy, negativity, and compliance which our society champions. What does that mean? In simple terms, it means you must have the strength to stand up for who you are and in what you believe.

How we respond to failures, disappointments, and adversity will determine how readily we achieve our short and long term goals. For those with a low tolerance for anything but success, the prognosis is not good. If you get down when your goals seem unreachable, don't despair. There are many sources of motivation. If you're a sports fan, consider that Michael Jordan was cut from his high school team. Wade Boggs was a late-round draftee who wound up in the Hall of Fame. Think of the so-called 'Cinderella' teams in the NCAA Basketball tournament that defeat the higher-touted Goliaths like UCLA, Kansas, Duke, etc. In politics, how about Barack Obama? Think he was born into a trust fund or political family? Hardly.

In the context of court proceedings, I can tell you the process is fundamentally imperfect. If you quiver when a nasty court official snarls at you for filing the wrong paper, it would help to think of this imperfection theory. Many times, too numerous to count in fact, I've been chided by an angry clerk for allegedly filing improper paperwork. On the occasion where he or she is correct, I'll merely re-file the appropriate papers with a smile and a laugh. When I'm in the right, I'll maintain my good humor and find a happier clerk.

There are other types of setbacks you'll be dealt both by the court and the administrative systems which will require continued optimism and faith in yourself. The opposition may prevail in motions for temporary things. The ultimate success, though, comes from winning the final hearing or trial or in negotiating a settlement. If you get too caught up in such initial proceedings, you'll lose sight of the fact that they are inconsequential.

Self-confidence, feeling good about yourself, and enduring disappointing results are inter-dependent concepts and essential components of effective self-advocacy. Think about this for a second. Wouldn't you agree that you're less susceptible to moods and being influenced by circumstances and people when, at your core, you feel happy? The question then becomes: How does one capture and maintain good feelings?

That's quite a subjective question, so I'll answer it in kind, hoping that your experiences may be similar to mine in some fashion. I believe happiness and joy come from humility, a lack of entitlement or expectation, and a respect for all people. Feeling good should be a regular occurrence, independent of how good or bad your day was. It should also be free of the burdens and temptations of materiality. We have all heard someone condition happiness on money (e.g. "If only I were wealthy, things would be so much easier"). Often, rich people have more severe problems than those who live off weekly paychecks.

My experiences have proven that making money is connected to how we feel. Would you hire a lawyer who lacked confidence in himself? Doubtful. When I graduated from law school, I now realize that I wasn't feeling very good about myself. Instead of rejoicing in my future and celebrating the qualities which distinguished me from the swarms of law students who graduated with me, I bought into the fear game. Fear that I was too inexperienced, fear that there were not enough jobs out there, and so forth.

It's amazing how you can talk yourself out of just about anything. That's what I did by selling myself short. I settled for an associate position in a disreputable firm working for an unsavory crackpot of an attorney. Languishing in such an unhealthy work environment sapped my self-esteem. Maybe you've been in one of these situations before. You start to make excuses because you're ashamed. You minimize your poor choice to continue working there and say your boss is "not so bad" even though you know in your heart that he's the scourge of life. To do other than lie would be admitting you are either too weak or foolish (or both) to work at a sweat shop. It would take a strong person to admit such a mistake.

WARM-UP

In my case, I had an epiphany of sorts where I convinced myself that there was another way, a better way, and that I was worthy of a better outcome. Having worked for others throughout my adult life, I opted to open my own law office and have embraced the excitement of each day. Some people are not so fortunate. Perhaps their rut is so deep and pronounced that hope is impossible, so they settle for far less than they desire. Maybe people and circumstances have broken their will to a point where they don't believe they deserve better. Sad.

As I say, I was a lucky one. Once I took that big, initial step of self-determination and independence, the other steps since then have been smaller and easier. We've all had adversities to shape us. I believe they can hurt you, if you so permit, or help if you make that choice. You must figure out how to take that first step of self-determination, to confront fear, your inner demons, and perhaps all of that negative self-talk which has accumulated in some people as tartar does in the teeth of those who fail to brush. Without a plan to take that necessary step the remainder of this book may be rendered meaningless.

So how do you conquer fear?

What a challenging question to answer. If it weren't, then there'd be no need for therapists, coaches, or experts. Let's take a stab. The most important starting place, I believe, is to clear the past and to avoid dwelling on the future. Think about the present. When I question choices I made years ago or anticipate what may happen in the next year, next month, or even tomorrow, I start feeling anxious. Why? For one, those events are out of our control. For another, our memory of those past events or preparation for future events is often distorted. That is, we imagine them, instinctively, to have been worse then they were. Our minds are interesting things, the way they can go off in different directions. The good thing is that we have control over our thoughts, and therefore our happiness.

The other point I want to stress, as we complete our warm-up, is that fear really paralyzes you at two distinct times: Before you take the proverbial leap of faith and when your initial attempt is disappointing. The second instance is equally potent. What do we say to ourselves when events and people frustrate us? Do we blame and make excuses? Worse still, do we quit in the face of a setback or two?

To weave these concepts into our subject matter, will you dismiss your eviction case against a hellacious tenant if a clerk snaps at you for filing the wrong paperwork? What about bullying state troopers? Do they speak the Gospel? Will you fight back (not physically, of course, but through the legal system) if they over-step?

The answers to these questions depend on you. You can succeed in self-advocacy if you so desire. To paraphrase the prophetic words of Abraham Lincoln: "Your determination to succeed is the single greatest factor in your success."

Go for it! Now's the time. Forget about what anyone may think and simply believe in yourself.

PART I

MAXIMIZING NEGOTIATION

Now, before starting our substantive discussion, I ask that you consider the sub-title I've chosen: 'Maximizing Negotiation'. Think about what I'm getting at by sticking 'maximizing' in front of 'negotiation'. Give up? I'm making a point of the finite and imperfect nature of negotiation. It doesn't always work. Sometimes, lack of success is the fault of circumstance, but often poor technique is to blame. Take advantage of the opportunity which negotiations afford. People often associate effective negotiation with lawyers, and for a good reason. If you picked up the paper on any given day, my guess is that you would find no fewer than five high profile cases in which lawyers are trying to negotiate a settlement. In fact, millions of other cases are settled in private on a regular basis.

But many lawyers are ill-equipped for effective negotiation. They may be too uptight, poor-tempered, or disillusioned as to the task. That may not surprise you. A fancy law degree and an extensive vocabulary can hinder achieving an advantageous deal. In the case of insurance defense lawyers, their clients have billions of dollars and are often prepared to spend hundreds of thousands on litigation. Consequently, these lawyers usually prefer protracted, inefficient proceedings as opposed to negotiated settlements.

More to the point, each of us (non-lawyers and lawyers alike) negotiates on a regular basis. We negotiate use of the bathroom during peak hours with our significant others. We negotiate the purchase of a house, a car, or a lawnmower. We negotiate or dispute a charge on our cable bill which we feel is too high. We negotiate or challenge a grade we receive from a teacher or professor.

In some situations, we want something intangible. For example, assume you have been dating someone for a while and are meeting his or her friend for the first time. Making a favorable impression is likely important. In a sense, you must negotiate your likeability to the friend and persuade that friend that you are right for the person you are pursuing. You will need to apply the skills we will discuss in this section.

Another example is a job interview. The interviewer has something you need, namely a job. Your quest is to persuade him or her that you are the most qualified candidate for the position. You may have a sterling resume and influential people who recommend you, but if you fail to effectively negotiate your merits during the interview, do you think you will be offered the job?

How do you get what you want? Isn't that the objective of negotiation? If I could answer that question in a word, paragraph, or a page, there would be no need for this discussion. For that matter, the scores of other books, articles, and lectures which have attempted to de-mystify negotiation would be equally unnecessary.

Furthermore, since so much has been written on the subject, approaches vary as to how you get what you want through negotiation. Certain of these books are featured on law school syllabi, while others were penned by famous authors. My intention here is **not** to undercut any of these works or to claim that my ideas are better. You will also note, in reading this section, that some of the principles propounded are time-tested truisms that have been practiced since Biblical times. It would be

PART I

impossible to address such a common subject matter with all new theories.

There is, however, a unique element to this discussion. While thinking like a lawyer (something of which non-lawyers are more than capable) is essential in the pre-negotiation part of the process, the reverse holds true. Thinking and acting too much like a lawyer may hurt the negotiation process itself. This premise may seem cryptic, particularly for those who are non-lawyers. But it is quite simple. Analyzing the circumstances of the negotiation, the parties involved, and exactly what you want requires skills we frequently associate with lawyers. You need to investigate, research, and prepare in this phase of the process. The difficult work, in my view, must be completed before the actual negotiations begin. As daunting as the task may seem, non-lawyers are capable.

Obviously not every negotiation requires hours of preparation. Some opportunities to negotiate present themselves with little or no warning. As we lawyers would say, there are general rules and then exceptions to these general rules. Assume for now that we are dealing only with the general rule that a window for preparation is available.

Do you need a law degree to master these techniques and reap the financial and health benefits of effective negotiation? No. I've practiced law for fifteen years, so I speak from experience. My training and work as a self-employed attorney have exposed me to numerous negotiations. I have noted techniques which have failed and ones which have worked. The toughest part about effective negotiation is transcending one's own needs to the needs of the other person. When you enter the negotiation phase, your ability to connect and personalize your presentation is vital, as we will discuss. Comforting the other person and making genuine expressions of understanding for his or her concerns must be paramount.

Why is this so tough? For one, in our microwave, capitalist society, success is associated with vanquishing the opponent.

THE LAWYER WITHIN

There is a winner and a loser. We see it in sports, in high profile court cases, and in Hollywood. Further, we often lionize the individual who refuses to compromise his position in achieving success. Take the case of a baseball manager who constantly fights with the team owner, the critics, and the conventional wisdom with regard to his managerial decisions (in other words refusing to negotiate). If the team wins, he's a hero. If they lose, he'll get fired. Our society loves a fighter, someone willing to sacrifice all that matters to him or her, repudiating public opinion in an effort to beat the opponent.

For another, we are often too needy at the time of negotiation to spend much, if any, time evaluating the other person's position. The challenge then is to focus on the larger picture, namely how an effectively-negotiated deal can benefit us. Getting to that point requires a letting-go of the demands of our egos.

The other challenging component to effective negotiation is the fact that few people understand the process. Some types sabotage a successful deal by over-lawyering. They're the Perry Masons of negotiation, only they lose sight of the fact that Perry Mason's style, while brilliant in front of a jury, often fails in negotiation sessions. These individuals, often-disgruntled lawyers, try to humiliate and overwhelm opponents to submission. They research their cases, pay scrupulous attention to detail and argue with vigor. They may cite studies, statistics, and articles written by renowned specialists in the particular area.

It feels good as they hammer each point, knocking down their opponent's position. "I'm right, you're wrong" is essentially what they're saying. What's the problem with this approach? After all, if they can back their views with credible facts and sources wouldn't that prove their ultimate conclusions? A simple appreciation of human nature reveals the obvious flaws in this method. The dynamic of a zero sum game (e.g. a winner and a loser) works well in a trial in front of a neutral fact-finder consisting of a judge or jury. Where the other side is in essence your fact-finder, beating him or her down with what you consider to be the truth serves no interest other than puffing your ego.

Now, if you agree with my premise that successful negotiation mandates an understanding of and respect for the views of the other side, the Perry Mason approach will fail. Perry Mason only wins in court. Instead, listen to what your opponent has to say. Never dismiss or minimize his or her opinions no matter how unfounded they may seem. You will not compromise your opinions by understanding those of your opponent. Playing a game of legal 'gotcha' may pump your adrenaline for the moment, but you will fail in the long term. You can take the steam out of other folks' passionate opinions and soften them for a negotiated agreement by simply catering to their egos. Think about how good you feel when someone listens to you speak for two minutes without interruption. My guess is you feel validated and, dare I say, special.

Prepare like a lawyer but negotiate like a human being.

A. The Work of a Lawyer in Negotiations

For those who are not lawyers, it is important to have a perspective on how negotiation plays out in the legal world. How else can you know when and when not to implement lawyer-like skills in the negotiation process? If you are expecting me to explain the two hundred thirty year evolution of American Jurisprudence, you will be disappointed. What follows is less than an introduction to the referenced subject matter; it is a mere taste.

The other danger in attacking such a general topic in one chapter is the reality that the law profession is so diverse. The work of a corporate lawyer differs markedly from that of a public defender. One handles multi-million dollar transactions while the other may negotiate a plea agreement for an accused pedophile. Throw into the mix the work of government lawyers, small firm attorneys and non-practicing lawyers. You can see the problem.

So I'll pick merely one example to illustrate my point. Since I'm a self-employed lawyer, I'll choose a situation with which I've dealt. Say I am representing someone who has been seriously injured in a car accident. When the person has finished receiving necessary treatment, known as a medical end result, I'll send a demand package to the insurance company in an attempt to settle the case. The insurance company's modus operandi is clearly to pay out as little as possible on each claim. If they think there is any merit to the claim, they might make an initial, low-ball offer. There is a practical element to their madness. They realize if their cost to settle a case is $5,000 while the legal fees they would incur in litigating the claim might approach $10,000, a victory in the latter instance would be a financial loss. Then, I call back the adjuster and slightly lower my demand.

There are two main factors which will greatly influence whether I can settle the case: the facts and the disposition of the adjuster. If I have strong facts (i.e. clear liability of the person who hit my client and extensive injuries,) I'm in good shape. Now, if I have good facts and a lenient adjuster, I may be able to set my price. The other extreme, of course, is bad facts and an ill-tempered adjuster.

If my luck falls somewhere in the middle, which is the likely scenario, then I need to prepare for possible settlement. This is where being a lawyer comes in. If negotiation fails or appears headed in that direction, lawyers know how to file lawsuits. The threat of a lawsuit will often break a deadlock. Why? Defending a lawsuit is expensive. Both parties know that. They also know that my fee is contingent, so I don't get paid more to do extra work. It stands to reason that most injury lawyers are reluctant to file lawsuits on these cases. Therefore, the adjusters are aware that many lawyers will back down when the case has a value of three thousand dollars or less. These lawyers think it's not worth the effort, not to mention the filing fee of a few hundred dollars

PART I

to get the case in court.

You may initially think this reasoning makes sense. But, whether you are a lawyer negotiating an injury case or a non-lawyer negotiating a charge on a telephone bill, your approach should be similar. Here's the key piece to increasing the probability of getting what you want: Show the other side that you are prepared to fight and that you'll likely win unless your opponent compromises. In bare terms, therein lies the essence of a lawyer's contribution to negotiations. I keep this principle in mind when a wronged consumer calls. He or she will talk about suing his or her landlord, car dealer, etc. The person will stress how he or she has limited resources for litigation and wishes to put the matter behind them as soon as possible. In other words, he or she wants me to threaten/bluff suing the other side, in the hope of obtaining a settlement. Most of the time this is a failing strategy. You can't assume you will be able to negotiate if you need to do so, a concept we'll discuss in the upcoming section.

Returning to our example of a personal injury case, how do we negotiate? Begin by researching your options when you are at a stalemate. On occasion, I have gone above the adjuster and spoken directly with his or her supervisor. Sometimes this approach works. If the supervisor feels this associate adjuster has been unreasonable, it's possible he will increase the offer. On occasion, though, his blind loyalty to his 'team player' will carry the day, and he will support his or her offer. Trying to convince the supervisor otherwise will likely frustrate you. At worst, he'll hang up the phone and terminate the process.

The next step is to contemplate sending a written demand alleging the insurance company has engaged in unfair settlement practices. In Massachusetts, there is a specific statute which proscribes such conduct and sets a penalty of triple damages if a court determines such was the case. Proving unfair settlement practices is quite different from merely alleging it in a demand letter. Nonetheless, the infusion of bargaining power can be remarkable. How would you feel if you were an insurance adjuster and a lawyer sent a well-written letter detailing how you had conducted your job in an unfair manner? Might they not look at the daunting possibility of added exposure and throw another thousand dollars or so on top of their previous settlement offer? The answer is 'yes'; it happens all the time.

The last resort, of course, is litigation. Let's face it: We live in a sue-happy society. You often hear people exclaim, "I'm calling my lawyer" in response to every perceived wrong. Those who have never been through the court process are invariably disillusioned about what's involved. People speak confidently of wanting their proverbial day in court. But it is far from a simple process. Their 'day' is more likely months or years. A complicated medical malpractice case, for example, can take upwards of five years to come to trial from the day it is filed in court. As one judge wisely said, "Due Process is not a perfect process." In other words, even if you feel you have a great case, the court process rarely goes according to expectations. It is often long and unpredictable. In that regard, though life and death stakes are not involved, it is like war. Those who are too quick to file lawsuits are shortsighted. Moreover, they often have had little practical experience with and exposure to litigation.

That said, returning to our example, if the insurance company's offer to settle is zero or unfairly low, your only viable option may be litigation. The lawyer prepares a complaint and files it in the appropriate court. This act injects another party into the equation, the defense counsel who represents the insured. In some instances, the ministerial act of commencing the litigation process may engender new settlement discussions.

Unfortunately, most of the time it does not. You must push by filing written discovery, taking depositions, and the like. In a contingent case, where economy of time matters, this is particularly vexing. If you spend fifty hours on discovery and another fifty on trial prep and the actual trial, you can see the problem. At two hundred fifty dollars an hour, the average billing rate for a Boston lawyer, you've spent twenty-five thousand dollars worth of your time. The upside of what you're fighting for better be a least two times that figure.

So to conclude, a non-lawyer is well-served to appreciate the litigation process. When you are negotiating in life, you will maximize your chances of success by approaching certain aspects of the process with a lawyer's eye. As we will discover in subsequent chapters, though, at times in negotiation you should refrain from acting like a lawyer.

B. The Advantages of Effective Negotiation

Let's take a step back. Please indulge me for a moment. We're going to talk a bit about what negotiation means and the benefits you can reap from it. Sound third-gradish? Give me a chance to convince you otherwise.

1. Health and Happiness

Particularly for men, our culture encourages confrontation. If someone wrongs you, fight back. Don't sit and take it or worse yet, try to make a deal. What are you, a sissy? Plus, what do most men in television commercials look like? They're strong and self-assured. Standing up for yourself and fighting for your beliefs is in large measure the American way. Is it a coincidence that a large percentage of men sit in front of their televisions every Sunday to root for their football team? They cheer when there is a touchdown or defensive hit.

Well, in the world of negotiation, confrontation, pride, and chauvinism fail. Moreover, in the sphere of good health, such measures fail as well. Too much stress ratchets up your blood pressure exposing you to a slew of mental and physical ailments. You don't need a fancy medical degree to know that. It follows, then, that effective negotiation benefits your health. You're at peace with the natural world and community of human beings. Making an agreement and resolving a dispute without resorting to fighting keeps blood pressure down. You need not be a doctor to know that low levels of stress decrease the risk of heart disease and other major illnesses. That's not to suggest that no stress is good. At that point, life would be boring and meaningless.

Continuing with what some may consider an over-simplification, would you not agree that good health leads to happiness, which in turn leads to better relationships? Who wants to be around a pill or an irritant? If you're angry, contentious, and self-righteous, you will likely turn away good people who would otherwise rally for you.

2. Goodwill and Reputation

Remember that in spite of what some people may say, we are all sensitive. The degree of our sensitivity is the only variable. No one likes to feel wrong, stupid, silly or defeated. Have you ever known someone who, when aggressively confronted, submits with words to the effect of, "You are right and I am wrong?" Of course not, unless they're under duress or victims of low self-esteem. Therefore, even if you achieve a short term gain with your zero-sum-game mentality, you'll have a bruised ego and likely made an enemy.

So then when your name comes up in a conversation that your vanquished opponent has with others, what do you think he'll say about you? Good things? Never. Even if in your prior dealings with him you were absolutely in the right, he will not remember the substance. What he will remember is how you made him feel inadequate and wrong in some way. In the words of Maya Angelou, "I've learned that people will forget what you said, people will forget what you did, but people will never forget how you made them feel." Of course, your opponent didn't think he was wrong so he'll spread negative things about you to other people. You may think that it is silly to try to control what others say about us, but even as an optimist who believes that people are mostly good and won't slander you for no reason, I've learned that people do slander others for no reason, so it is imperative that you try to control what others think and say about you, at least in a business context. The simple point is that having a reputation as a reasonable, fair person who fights as a last resort is a very good thing. You can guess by now where I am going here— being fair and reasonable fosters good relationships and nurtures your soul and your wallet in the process. Remember that your approach to negotiations should be long-term. Think of the work of a smart real estate broker. If he lists a property for a seller, do you think he forgets about the buyer after the closing? Worse yet, do you think he would ever alienate the buyer during the pendency of the deal? Of course not. He wants the buyer to list with him when he sells.

However, you may also challenge my premise. You may feel that being too conciliatory will foster a reputation as a 'softie' or a 'wimp'. Alternatively, in the law and in life, being viewed as tough or privileged will win you many friends, clients, and admirers. I agree with both of those statements.

There is an implication in these challenges, however, with which I adamantly disagree. Being conciliatory is not tantamount to being soft. As I've already said and will address at length later on, if your opponent in negotiations is not being reasonable don't make the deal. Walk away. Wimpy people disgust me. Wimpiness and reasonableness reside in different planets.

Therefore, if you are reputed as a sensible person who puts productivity above his or her ego and above agenda, you will grow your contacts and your happiness. As we'll see later on, not every situation is negotiable. Approaching potential conflict with an open mind and willingness to listen is a theme of this book.

3. Financial

An obvious financial gain from negotiation concerns time. Plainly said, you'll have more of it. Negotiation resolves issues on a short or long term basis, meaning you can allocate time and energies to other projects, activities, or for rest and relaxation. Swift resolution means you will not need to spend time in protracted negotiations or proceedings. In business, where time is money, saving the former means increasing the latter.

Conversely, the inability to reach a negotiated accord means a stalemate. In certain instances, such a result is unavoidable. Not every situation can be negotiated to settlement. Where that stalemate is avoidable, failure to negotiate effectively will result in a financial loss for which you can blame yourself.

To see how this plays out, let's use our example from the previous section. Let's say that the insurance company has made a semi-reasonable offer to settle your personal injury claim. Say they've put ten thousand on the table, and you think the case is worth twenty to twenty-five thousand. If you spurn their offer and put the case in suit, the insurance company obviously will not pay you ten thousand while disputing responsibility for the remaining fifteen. This means that you have to invest the requisite few hundred dollars to file a complaint and that you must see the court process through. If you're lucky, the defense lawyer may offer to settle in a few months for, say, twelve and a half to fifteen thousand dollars. In that case, your risk will have paid off.

There's a good chance, based on the facts in this example, that your rejection of the semi-reasonable offer will prove to have been a poor decision. Here's why: Filing suit requires an immediate cost of the filing fee (typically between two hundred and three hundred fifty dollars) and service of the summons and complaint (another forty to fifty dollars). If the case does not settle at the initial stages, you must contend with additional expenses such as deposition costs. At the final stage, another wave of expenses kicks in. You will need to subpoena witnesses and possibly pay for expert witnesses, depending on the case.

The aforementioned out-of-pocket costs are more of a financial annoyance. The real cost is time. Whether you settle a contingent case after ten hours of work or five hundred hours of work is a significant difference, don't you think? Well, once you put your auto-accident case in suit, your time expenditure will increase dramatically. In addition to preparing and filing the complaint, you'll have to contend with preparing interrogatories, other written discovery, and responding to said discovery from the defense counsel. Trial preparation and trial obviously represent the case's climax and are time-heavy.

As an aside, I've encountered several head-strong clients who, faced with the options of settling for less than face value or pursuing litigation, do a curious dance. At first, they trumpet their Due Process right to a jury trial and talk about justice and fairness. They might also mock the offer as ridiculous or insultingly low, even though objectively that is not the case. What's interesting is that, without exception in my experience, these types will quickly compromise their moral high ground when faced with the financial practicalities of protracted litigation. What's my point? The cost of rejecting reasonable offers of settlement, when properly explained, can persuade even the most stubborn person to negotiate and compromise.

C. Analyzing the Situation

Now we're ready to really begin. You're in the game. A negotiable situation has presented itself. It may be as simple as a dispute with your spouse over who watches the children on a particular evening or more complicated, such as a land boundary disagreement with your neighbor. Certainly if faced with the former scenario your preparation time is limited.

For the purpose of our discussion, let's assume you have some preparation time. The first question to ask and answer is: What are your objectives? Sometimes this is easy to ascertain. In the example of who watches the children, your goal is either to watch or not watch the children. Other times, your feelings and desires will take more time to process. If you've experienced problems, not of your making, with your cell phone and you seek recompense from your phone company, you may not have an immediate financial figure in mind. So in that example, it would be helpful to think about a specific number you think is fair before making the phone call. Otherwise, you undercut your negotiating power by coming across as unsure of your position.

In many instances, your opponent may attempt to rush the resolution process. To the extent you can, I suggest you stall until you are clear on your objectives. We frequently see this dynamic play out in the context of promotions. For example, in my law practice I will annually get calls from marketing agencies promoting 'special deals'. This offer is open, they say, for a short period of time.

Knowing what you want is related to negotiating from a place of strength. The key here is confidence, to be distinguished from its evil cousin—arrogance. We've all seen bravado in people, and it turns us off. Would you be inclined to negotiate with someone who floats in his or her own cocoon of self-indulgence? I guess 'no'. Neither would I. On the other hand, maintaining a simple and humble belief in yourself and in your position with respect to the issue at hand will enhance your bargaining position.

Sometimes your position may be somewhat flexible. In these instances, it is important to know exactly where your breaking point in the negotiation lies. If you are initially unable to ascertain this juncture, I suggest you step away from the situation and really think about your objectives. Too often, people approach negotiations with haste. In so doing, they compromise their bargaining power and agree on terms inconsistent with what they want.

D. Your Opponent in Negotiations

I have to be careful in using 'opponent' in this context. Remember that in negotiations, you must avoid playing so-called zero sum games; that is, your focus should be on crafting mutually-beneficial agreements, ones in which both sides win. If we were in the political arena, I'd say to avoid partisanship.

That said, you are opposing the other side insofar as you need something from that person. Were I to use 'partner' instead, that would improperly suggest there is no dispute between the two parties. Where many people fall short, however, is understanding and analyzing the needs and personality of the other person. I am far from the first person to ever make this declaration: We are all motivated by self-interest. Along the same lines, my grandfather made a proclamation to the effect of: "The world doesn't owe you anything." For those who play the 'why me?' pity card, I'm afraid their fate is transparent. If you expect people to give you what you want, as countless individuals do, you will waste your life waiting for an impossible result. Then, when that reality plays out, the pity types feel vindicated, saying, "See, I knew he/she would screw me."

Who is this person with whom you are negotiating? What are his or her likes and dislikes, dreams and fears, hobbies and interests? Is he or she reserved or outgoing? Spouse? Children? Sports fan? Once you can paint somewhat of a picture of this person, you'll immediately increase your bargaining power. Why? To paraphrase Dale Carnegie in his classic book, *How to Win Friends and Influence People,* by understanding a person and showing a genuine interest in his life, you'll ingratiate that person. Who doesn't like to feel special and valued, not to mention 'understood'? I have found that the most interesting people are those who are the most interested. People who attempt to understand my world are folks I want participating in my world, folks with whom I might share my thoughts and opinions on a variety of subjects.

In instances when you know the person with whom you are negotiating, sometimes intimately, you will not need to spend much time at this stage. Obviously, you know the tendencies of a spouse or family member better than you would a business associate. Other times, your opponent may be someone you have never met, so your pre-negotiation analysis will be based on information from other people, reports or other written material.

Sometimes, merely knowing your opponent will be a deal-breaker. What if you start talking to him and notice signs of mental illness. Say he starts verbally abusing you or saying disparaging things, which make you feel uncomfortable. Without even getting to the substance of the discussion, you may need to end the discussion. A person's bad reputation, if revealed by reliable sources, may terminate the negotiation in the same fashion.

At the other end of the spectrum are the easy and accommodating personalities. Given their comforting demeanor and perhaps aversion to confrontation, they're inclined to want to make a deal. Unlike their verbally-deceptive counterparts, these folks are complementary and gentle. It is not hard to work with them. Sometimes, the good reputation of an opponent in negotiations can facilitate an agreement. Robert E. Lee, the famed Southern general during the Civil War, said he signed the surrender agreement at the Appomattox Court House in large measure because of his respect for President Lincoln. He had never met Lincoln but knew of Lincoln's kind reputation as someone who would treat the vanquished Southern states with fairness and dignity. Can you imagine the potential historical consequences had Lincoln not assumed a conciliatory posture? The war may have lasted several more years, causing more destruction and loss of life.

Everyone else is in the grey area. With some people, as the cliché goes, you'll be a bee with honey. Others, though, respond better to an initial showing of firmness. Many men are interested in sports, so you may comfort them by broaching that topic. The key is to encourage your opponent to speak as much as possible. That way you have a very clear idea of what he wants. Here's a quote I keep in my office: "It is the dull man who is always sure, and the sure man who is always dull." H.L. Mencken, a famous American author and journalist of the Nineteenth and Twentieth Centuries, wrote those words. They ring true in negotiations and in life. If you rejoice too much in the sound of your own voice you will likely disinterest the person with whom you are speaking. You need not be a master of logic to deduce that a disinterested person is disinclined to open up about matters of concern in his or her life. In the world of negotiations, such a misstep may cost you greatly.

E. Preparation

Once you've analyzed the situation and your opponent, you should have a fair idea of what's involved. As discussed, the dynamic may be such that you conclude no viable agreement can be reached and you walk away at this preliminary stage. In all other instances, you must forge ahead.

The famed Supreme Court Justice Louis Brandeis, paraphrasing the words of John Adams, said, "Facts, facts, facts: give me facts." Ostensibly, in his court, substance ruled over style. The same approach applies to negotiations. To achieve a maximum result you will need to make your case, though in a more gentle manner, to your opponent. Fancy clothes, sweet-talking, compliments, and the like have a place in this process. They are not the bedrock, though. As Justice Brandeis said, the facts and circumstances govern.

It makes sense that a thorough understanding of the facts must be requisite for any effective negotiation session. Before addressing the process of preparation in negotiation, let's talk a bit about emotions and where they fit in. You've heard the cliché 'Don't shop when you're hungry', haven't you? An analogous phrase would apply in the world of negotiation: Don't negotiate when your emotions are charged. When you're feeling too emotional, you're liable to make poor decisions.

Let's see how this plays out, using the example of purchasing a car. If ever there were a business where price is flexible, it is the auto industry. So, say you want a compact car, preferably a convertible that gets good mileage. A Volkswagen Cabrio, my wife's former car, comes to mind. You go to the dealer knowing what you want and how much you're willing to spend. To sweeten the prospects, let's assume you have transacted in the past with this particular dealer, meaning your chance of dropping the price is presumably higher.

Sounds great, huh? Well, life is rarely perfect, so let's inject a wild card: You had a major dental procedure just prior to your visit to the dealer and you're in some discomfort. Add to that the fact that the procedure was quite costly. In short, you're in a foul mood.

The dealer greets you with a smile, abruptly ending his small talk with a crony. He knew you were coming, so he's prepared with a number of Cabrios to show you. You say no to his offer of coffee as you look at the first vehicle in his showroom. My guess is that the negotiation will soon break down, leaving both parties feeling disappointed.

Why? The simple answer is that you are too preoccupied with unresolved emotional baggage from the dentist situation to effectively concentrate on the task at hand. You are not in the calm, detached mental place which is conducive to making sound decisions. To use another analogy, a person ending one relationship would be well served to reinvent himself through a period of alone time prior to starting up with someone new. Otherwise, he risks bringing unresolved issues into the new relationship.

The next logical question is: What do you do if you don't have the time to work off those feelings? Well, this book is not a primer on meditation, stress relief, or the like. I'm simply not experienced enough in those areas to provide competent counsel. That said, my suggestion is to explore activities and methods which help clear your head, depending on how much time you have. If you need assistance in this regard, there are scores of books on the subject. In some cases, seeking professional counsel in the form of a psychiatrist or psychologist makes sense.

Let's get back to preparation. When I was in high school, I believed that performance was determined exclusively by the quantity of my preparation. You could say I was a concrete thinker. If I studied ten hours for a history exam, I expected that I'd be a cinch for an 'A'. On occasion this theory worked, but often it did not. Why? Well, the quality of my studying, as I learned in later years, was determinative. Three hours of intensive study work more effectively than do ten hours of study in front of the television.

In preparing for negotiation, the same principle applies in equal force. If you are seeking to purchase a car and want a Toyota, does it make much sense to research the Blue Book values of Mercedes vehicles? Of course not. If you are a prospective new tenant, spending a half-hour in conversation with an existing tenant in the building which you want to rent will be more valuable than wading through ownership documentation concerning the building.

In short, preparation should be focused and goal-oriented. Once you've ascertained your objective, stream-line your preparation time to maximize results. First, make sure you are certain about what you want and need from this negotiation. Know what you absolutely won't budge on and what terms you are willing to accept, but remember to keep these expectations reasonable. Obtain any and all necessary forms that you need so that everything is properly documented on paper. Next, conduct research to find information that backs up your points and refutes your opponent's points. Do not waste time preparing extraneous information (e.g. do not research 15 cases to back up your points, one or two would be sufficient. Focus on the facts of your case, not on irrelevant information). Be sure you have a clear idea of which information to bait the other party with and which information to keep as your 'Ace in the Hole' in case you need to use it later on to give yourself the upper hand.

It's helpful to have the strengths of your position in bullet-point form so they are readily accessible in case your memory fails. In sum, it is imperative to embark on the preparation segment of negotiation by preparing as if you may have to enter into formal dispute resolution on short notice.

Some of the best deals/agreements I've ever made have taken a long time to achieve. Do not expect quick success. Rather, be prepared for protracted dealings in which the initial results may be disappointing.

F. Battle Mentality

You may sense hypocrisy in my subtitle to this section. After all, on the one hand I stress conciliation and on the other, I opt to use the word 'battle'.

Let me respond with the following: Merely because you 'plan' for battle does not necessarily mean you fight. It means only that you 'prepare' to fight. More times than not, when your opponent believes you have a strong 'case' (excuse me for sounding like a lawyer) he will soften his demands. Of course, as we will discuss in greater detail later on, the presentation of your knowledge is vital. Overplaying your proverbial hand will compromise the advantage gained through preparation.

How does this work? For one, while your ultimate goal will be reaching a mutually-advantageous agreement, you need to prepare to fight. When your opponent sees how strong your hand is, she will be more inclined to resolve the matter.

Assume that your negotiations will be strenuous, long, and perhaps frustrating at times. That way you will not be disappointed if, to some degree, they are.

PART I

G. At the Table: Poor Negotiations

I believe life is like a standardized test. An effective approach to challenges entails crossing off the wrong answers. Doing so uncovers creative options which are otherwise hidden. Therefore, we begin our discussion on the actual negotiation (which I've cutely referred to as "At the Table") by identifying and eliminating poor approaches.

Since negotiation is so wide-reaching and varied in complexity, examples work best in illuminating points. I like to pick ones that are common, so let's go with applying for a job. Your initial reaction may be to question how this involves negotiation. Let's assume the company to which you have applied appears inclined to hire you but has offered only a nominal salary. For the position to be viable, you will need to persuade them to increase their proposed wage.

I should add one more point before beginning our substantive discussion. Employment negotiations are unique in that, unlike buying a car or a house, the relationship endures.

1. Inactive Listening to the Other Side

Why is it we humans have such difficulty with this one? One reason might be that we live in a fast-paced society which underlines activity and aggressiveness. Another factor concerns the myth which goes like this: The more you talk, the stronger you make your case. Some people manifest nervousness by speaking with incoherence and voluminousness. A final answer might be ego, namely the ego of the person doing all of the talking. It feels good for him to be the centerpiece, the answer-man, the know-it-all. Memo to the ego-centric maniac: Your selfishness turns people away.

By entering the negotiation with a clear head, freed from the emotional encumbrances of which we've spoken, you'll find it easier to listen to the needs of the other side. So, when the prospective employer speaks of wanting to hire someone willing to relocate to another city if necessary, you won't gloss over that important piece of information. I become frustrated and annoyed when I feel the person to whom I am speaking is disinterested in or inattentive to what I have to say. No one likes having a one-sided conversation.

Poor listeners are not malicious. They may have limited social skills, insecurities or perhaps they see your supportive listening as an invitation to speak at length about their problems. In any event, they're a drain.

What are specific examples of inactive listening? If you've come to my car lot, expressing interest in a vehicle and I tout my prowess as a salesperson, will you be interested in buying from me? Of course not, you say. How obvious. Be careful, though, because self-absorption feels good. Unless you are aware and disciplined, you could slip into a trap which is sure to sabotage any successful negotiation.

Let's continue with another car sale example. Your prospect comes in, unsure of what kind of car she wants but certain of the need for a car. Let's also add that your prospect is gentle, soft spoken, and polite. That's a tempting fact-pattern for self-indulgence and ineffective listening for the undisciplined negotiator.

Let's say you are an undisciplined negotiator. You push the most expensive cars, the Saabs and Mercedes, hoping for a high sale. In the process you brag about how many of those cars you've recently sold. You're so consumed with feeding your own ego that you may miss clues your prospect drops. She may make reference to having young children or being concerned with getting good mileage. You're oblivious to these subtleties as you jabber away. If the person with whom you are negotiating is instead talkative, you'll have a different challenge--namely remaining focused on what she has to say. If she's talking about the welfare of her kids and you talk about the baseball game, it's likely you'll alienate her.

Now, back to the job example: you attend the second

interview determined to persuade the two company executives that you are the best person for the job. They seem reserved and eager to listen, encouraging you to prattle through the laundry-list of accomplishments you've committed to memory in the course of your preparation. The more questions they ask, the more detailed you become, culminating in a reference to your part as Tinker Bell in your high school performance of *Peter Pan*. That said, where your opponent in negotiations appears interested in trivial subjects, use common sense in broaching such topics.

Set your ego aside so you can attend to her interests.

2. Mechanical Mistakes

Here we're talking about non-verbal habits and idiosyncrasies, which, notwithstanding active listening and positive verbal interaction, can erode negotiation. Say you are on the other end of the car sale as the purchaser. If a salesperson shakes your hand to the point that it hurts, won't that turn you off? Alternatively, what if the person offers you a limp handshake? Having experienced both extremes, I can say they are equally off-putting.

In my view, an intense handshake or gesticulation makes me uncomfortable. It fails to convey warmth, compassion, or understanding, which are essential ingredients. It may mean the person is nervous, either too eager to close the deal or lacking confidence in him or herself, so he has to emphasize his toughness. Now, if the person has a slight speech impediment or physical disability, such as Tourette's syndrome, the rules don't apply. Why? The obvious answer is that Tourette's syndrome is uncontrollable, whereas an overzealous or limp handshake is remediable. If you're an intense person by nature, that's O.K. Just beware of the effect your eagerness and excitability may have on others. Consider practicing awareness, particularly in contexts where you are meeting people for the first time. Otherwise said, ease into these situations.

Eye contact is also important. The proverbially "shifty-eyed" person may be either insecure or deceptive. At a minimum, though, he often fails to connect with the person to whom he's speaking. Common sense should be injected here. Good eye contact is not tantamount to staring into someone's eyes without blinking for fifteen minutes. Instead of insecure or deceptive, you may be perceived as frightening. There's a movie called *Jesus of Nazareth* in which the character of Jesus never blinks his eyes, not even once. Clearly, the objective is to portray his intensity and supernatural characteristics. While the approach is successful in movies, it often fails in real life. The best approach, I believe, is to focus your eyes comfortably on the person to whom you're speaking. Smile and laugh when it feels comfortable. Turning away to collect your thoughts is O.K.

Bad posture can work against you in negotiations. The Three Bears analogy works here as it does with eye contact. Don't stand too slouched or too upright. Instead, stand in an easy natural posture. To do otherwise risks sending a message of either sloppiness or insecurity. In the same category as poor posture, and this is something of which I've been guilty on occasion, is stretching your legs, rotating your neck and/or cracking your knuckles. Remember that if the deal falls through because the parties can't agree in spite of their best efforts, that's O.K. To squander an opportunity due to carelessness or one of the mistakes discussed in this chapter is inexcusable. An analogy is a football team that loses to a lower-caliber team because it repeatedly fumbles and is assessed penalties. Use your common sense as a compass; if you crack your knuckles once no one will mind. I'm talking about doing it repeatedly.

Tone is tougher to monitor because we all have different natural voices. Otherwise said, some people speak lower than others. If you are fortunate enough to possess a gentle, melodious, or confident voice by nature, you're lucky. Conversely, if folks squint at the sound of your stridency when you engage in small talk or you receive frequent requests to speak louder, this is an area in which you must improve. Again, awareness, as opposed to its evil twin named denial, is vital here. Until you temper the intensity of your sound or project your voice, your ability to effectively negotiate suffers.

3. Appearance Issues

One might think that attire is a mere function of finances. If you don't have significant funds, you may therefore balk at the notion that you can improve in this department. But wait a minute. What does color coordinating a tie with a shirt have to do with money? Or wearing khakis and a button-down shirt, instead of jeans and a t-shirt, to an important meeting? Dressing appropriately, though somewhat a function of opinion, connotes seriousness and professionalism, not to mention the ever-important absence of immaturity.

Be mindful of dress requirements dictated by the circumstances of your negotiation session. In some instances, over-dressing undercuts your substantive goals. Say you're a financial planner, and you're meeting a prospective client at his beach house in Miami. If you're invited for an informal lunch and swimming, showing up in a suit may turn him off. He may judge you as being out of touch or as someone to whom he cannot relate.

Hygiene is another negotiating factor over which we have control. Let's be clear about something, though. I am not contending that having great hygiene in and of itself will make you a negotiating guru. What I am saying is that poor hygiene can and does detract from effective negotiation. It might surprise you to know that in my experience, the wealthiest people are often the most neglectful when it comes to hygiene. One of my millionaire clients showed up for appointments in my office, and worse, court hearings, smelling like onions, garlic, body odor, and the like. Would you choose to deal with someone like this? Grooming is a word which should not be limited to pets. People need to be mindful of brushing hair, clipping nails, and bathing on a regular basis. Yeah, yeah, yeah, you're saying. It seems like such common knowledge, right? So why do so many lawyers show up for hearings looking like they just woke up? I've known high-level managers who are oblivious to their body odor.

Maximize your negotiating position before even uttering a word!

H. At the Table: The More Effective Way

As a trial lawyer, you may feel I am a hypocrite for my pronouncements of civility, sensitivity, and active listening. After all, even those of us who do not spend much time in a courtroom know that trials are about winners and losers, vicious cross-examinations, and parties that despise each other. Yes, yes, and yes. As someone who's been through the often ugly and invariably flawed process, though, I am here to assure you that it doesn't need to be that way in real life. When it is, everyone loses. Besides, courtrooms are far from microcosms of everyday life, because of the rules of procedure which govern them.

Let's first talk about finding common ground. First, here's a disclaimer: This principle, like others propounded in this book, must not be viewed in isolation or as absolute. If you're interested in selling your house but for financial reasons you are unwilling to sell for less than $500,000, you cannot find common ground if a prospective purchaser will not budge above $475,000. In that situation, and many others, there is no viable deal, and the parties should shake hands and move on.

Continuing with the house-sale example, let's say the buyer is not crazy about paying more than $475,000 but you sense she would if properly enticed. Say she's concerned about going higher than that because she feels she'll have to pay at least $30,000 to $40,000 on repairs and renovations. If you've spent adequate time listening to and asking questions of her and/or her broker, you'll likely succeed in ascertaining her mind-set. So, according to these numbers, she's willing to pay up to

$515,000 as long as she doesn't have to put additional money into the house.

How can you find common ground to make this happen? If you're a skilled carpenter, perhaps you can do the work yourself. If not, your objective is to find someone to do whatever work is necessary for $15,000 or less. You may be successful in achieving this objective, but it's also quite possible all the contractors you speak with will quote numbers in excess of $15,000. If that's the case and neither party is flexible, there is no deal. At least you can draw comfort from the knowledge that you did what you could to reach a win-win resolution.

I believe it's important to understand what finding common ground does and does not mean. First, what does it not entail? If reaching an agreement requires you to compromise your principles or goals to such an extent that you feel uncomfortable, then you have gone too far. Excuse the cliché, but you will have lost the forest for the trees. No deal is ever worth the sacrifice of your integrity. Now, where these boundaries are drawn is a matter of subjectivity, varying from person to person. For that reason, it would be pointless for me to attempt to objectify a highly subjective issue.

Finding common ground does require proactivity. Studying (and memorizing in some instances) the other side's mindset is essential. Being creative and patient are also helpful in this process. The earlier example of the home sale illustrates this point. Topics explored in prior chapters interweave here. If you can prevent vanity from entering the fray, your chances of reaching a favorable resolution improve. I also believe that flexibility, to be distinguished from 'selling out', is a major component of this concept.

It sounds so simple, doesn't it? Then why do so many people run afoul here? I'll respond with more comparisons. Why do so many people eat junk food when it's so obviously bad for your health? Likewise, with regard to smoking, excessive drinking, overworking, etc. My point is that the thrill of the moment (or in the case of desperate negotiation, the fear of the moment) obstructs our perspective as to what's in our best interest.

Be careful then, of putting yourself in a position of desperation. If the issue is purchasing a home and you're in need of housing because the lease on your apartment is up, be wary. If you come to the negotiating table in dire need of purchasing the house in order to avoid homelessness, the other side will likely exploit this weakness. What are your options? One choice is to secure transitional housing before you enter negotiations to purchase a home. That way, you can avoid settling for a bad deal out of desperation.

If this option is unavailable or impracticable, then you may have to enter the negotiation without a realistic option of calling off the deal. The first obvious rule here is to avoid panic. Maybe your opponent is desperate. Or, perhaps your opponent has a conciliatory, kind-hearted disposition and will not capitalize on your weakness by insisting on an inflated price. In any scenario, the key is to slow down the process. Let the other side do most of the talking, so you can ascertain his or her objectives. The other advantage of slowing down the process is you avoid doing or saying something that might reveal your need to make the deal. The ancient concept of 'caveat emptor' ("buyer beware") applies to negotiations in the same way that it does to the purchases of cars, homes, or anything for that matter.

There's another concept, helpful in effective negotiations, which bears discussion: Preserving the other person's ego. You don't have to be a trial lawyer to enjoy the thrill of 'zinging' it to your opponent. Haven't you ever argued, whether with intensity or not, and made a point to which the other person could not respond? Then, as your confidence grows, you embellish your argument with more facts, perhaps a statistic or two. Feels good doesn't it? This is particularly true if the other person is a snotty, know-it-all type or someone who's made you look or feel bad on one or more occasion. Revenge has a limited half-life, but it can feel euphoric in the short-term.

PART I

What is the problem? You're merely responding to an aggressor, right? Isn't our system of government based on justice? Well here's the problem: By retaliating in the above-illustrated manner, you're about to make a deal—potentially a good deal—with the person who's wronged you. It may be the case that the other person is so morally-disoriented, venal, abrasive or whatever that a deal is not viable under any circumstance. Still, I maintain that revenge fails in all situations. Why? For one, the other person will bad-mouth you to every available listener. It's a safe bet that some of those negative info-recipients are at least moderately reasonable people who could be persuaded by what this jerk has to say about you. Some people, particularly those who have seen the jerk in action, will dismiss his gossip. True. However, why supply this toxic person, who likely has available free time, with ammunition against you? Even jerks have moral compasses which inhibit them from slandering others without cause. Well, some do anyway!

Another reason why I discourage retaliation is that it saps your energy. My guess is that like me, you feel exhausted after arguing with someone over what you later come to realize is a trivial issue. Similarly, think of all the effort, planning and emotion a cold-blooded plan for revenge requires. And to what end? You may succeed in vanquishing the jerk who wronged you, but what might you become in the process? You'll have less time for family, friends, work, hobbies, activities, etc. Is that a fair trade off? I'd say 'no'. Further, the intensity required to retaliate may affect your health, because you'll be organizing many negative and unkind thoughts during your process of revenge and your level of stress and anxiety will rise. The simple life pleasures that are proven to nurture our souls and abet our health, such as watching a rainbow or listening to the raindrops, will have exited from your world. In extreme cases, revenge may effectively change your personality. As such, you may transform from a kind and patient person, to an uptight, angry man or woman.

A third and final argument against revenge is that it often destroys the possibility of reconciliation, discussed in a subsequent section. Sound crazy? I might have thought so at one point. My experiences, particularly my professional ones, have proven otherwise. On at least two occasions, I had contentious relationships with opposing counsel in litigation cases. You may say that litigation is about fighting, a valid point, but these two cases entered another realm. In one of the cases, which received considerable media attention, the other lawyer threatened to report me to the Bar and to sue me individually on several occasions. He was an older and well-respected attorney, adding clout to his threats. I countered, seeking sanctions on a discovery matter in the case. In short, we detested each other. Some civility entered the proceedings many months later, perhaps because we both compromised our feelings of self-righteousness, and ultimately we settled the case. Had either of us allowed sentiments of revenge to absorb our pursuit of the case, I believe our clients interests would have suffered. Now I see the lawyer with whom I fought, and we stop to exchange pleasantries. From my perspective, we've bonded from the war we fought against each other and have developed a mutual respect. I have had subsequent matters with these lawyers and notice the level of cooperation and professionalism I am now accorded. Fighting fair and preserving my opponent's dignity have enhanced my future negotiating position.

This discussion leads me to the final point of this chapter, distinguishing retaliation from strong advocacy. The latter invariably garners the respect and, sometimes, the admiration of your opponents and is characterized by fair play and professionalism; the fight is never personal, contrasting with the retaliation mind-set. Strong advocacy and courage to rally for important principles are therefore catalysts of effective negotiation, while retaliation (its antithesis) destroys the prospect of agreements.

PART I

I. When and How to Walk

Life is imperfect. Some might say unfair, but I prefer 'imperfect'. Implementing the strategies discussed earlier will, in my view, increase your chance of reaching agreements. Even if you put yourself in a great bargaining position, that may not be sufficient. Accordingly, in such situations you will have to walk away from any possible agreement.

The first question is 'when'? Like many topics of discussion in this book, that is a matter of subjectivity. If you are asking me to answer, my best response would be as follows: Walk when you feel any further concession would compromise your sense of integrity. Otherwise said, walk when things do not feel right. If you have developed some self-understanding and can pause from the pressure of the situation, you should be able to know when things do not feel right. I cannot objectify or clarify this advice beyond those guidelines.

Before addressing the second and equally vital question of 'how', let us discuss what might cause your desire to stop negotiating. First of all, accept that you will be frustrated when negotiations break down. You have invested time, energy, and perhaps money in the hope of making a deal. You have also likely made some initial concessions after encountering resistance. Do not blame yourself, though blame often becomes the button everyone wants to press in these situations. If you went beyond what could be reasonably expected to make a deal, you have gone too far. Further, avoid self-defeating and counterproductive generalizations such as: "I knew it wouldn't work"; "Negotiation always fails"; and the like.

Perhaps your negotiating opponent's demands are too steep or are reasonable but your finances are such that you need to have certain requirements met in order to make the deal happen. Other possibilities include the personality of your opponent or a sudden change in your circumstances creating a lessened desire to negotiate.

How to walk from an 'unsuccessful' (a word preferable to 'failed') negotiation is, in my view, the greater challenge. Why is that? For one, your reputation should mean something to you. If you lose control, exchange expletives with your opponent, make snide or unprofessional remarks, or otherwise comport in a less-than-business like manner, you will compromise your good name. That may negatively affect your ability to negotiate successfully in the future. Further, as discussed earlier, a bad reputation impinges on your health and happiness by creating undue stress.

Drama works well in movies and on television shows, doesn't it? It's also entertaining when a baseball manager loses his temper over what he perceives to be a bad call. He proceeds to storm up to the umpire, throw his cap to the ground, kick dirt in front of him and bump up against him. The umpire gesticulates with his arms, yells back and then ejects the misbehaving manager. The fans roar; the television ratings sore; the manager pays a small fine and everyone returns to life as usual the next day when the teams play again. A good fight between hockey players can have the same effect.

In our lives, drama can be equally intriguing and provide a needed escape from stress and boredom—as long as we're not the actors. When we are the actors, drama is unproductive and leads others to gossip about us. We morph into comic figures or 'characters' which may make us popular in certain circles. It may also make us notorious and alienate us from colleagues. That's not the reputation you want as a negotiator.

So if kicking and screaming fails, the over-simplification is to be nice, a phrase that makes some people squeamish because it suggests you act nicely. Continuing with that reasoning, those squeamish souls detest the nice card the same way young children repulse vegetables. The obvious similarity is that in both instances the spawned item or behavior is beneficial.

But, before you harass me about how you always get burned

PART I

when you do the ethical thing or you subscribe to the principles etched by Machiavelli in *The Prince* hundreds of years ago, wait a moment. Allow me to first define how I believe you should respond when deal-making breaks down.

For one, I'm not recommending you apologize for or condone any misbehavior by your fellow negotiator. To do so would be emotionally dishonest and inappropriate. Most importantly, it would not be fair or comforting to you. Further, I'm also not encouraging you to pretend you're thrilled with the unsuccessful negotiations. Each of these routes represents the opposite of banging (your fist or someone's head) against a wall as you storm away. The ultimate question regarding this issue, simply put, is: How do you find the comfortable ground between an emotionally honest response and withdrawal/phoniness? My answer is that you must detach from your feelings and respond with brevity and directness. Don't waste the energy required by either extreme response. I believe that you'll feel better if you accept the unsuccessful negotiation. Give yourself credit for trying, and remind yourself that most negotiations, where you apply the discussed techniques, will succeed.

Announce to your opponent that the deal's off. I would advise you not to get into the particulars (e.g., you can't afford or live with the emotional/financial cost of the proposal, etc.). If you do so, you might make yourself feel worse or come off as attempting manipulation. If the other side questions you, be equally brief in saying you can't accept the terms as proposed. Don't be suckered if the other side attempts to manipulate or guilt you into changing your mind. Unless they substantively change their position, you must leave (in peace).

Walk away, depending on the nature of your communications. And of course, add a pleasantry as you depart.

Leave acting to the Hollywood people.

J. Re-Opening Negotiations

The up-side to living in a fast-paced society, where instant gratification reigns, is that a new day can often represent a new beginning. Applying this principle to the world of negotiations offers encouragement. We can appreciate the importance of 'walking' from negotiations with dignity and respect for your opponent. If you close the door too hard, you will have no opportunity to re-negotiate.

Let's be clear on something. My experiences highlight the fact that most negotiations that end the first time will either not be re-negotiated or will not succeed subsequent times. Why is that so? My instinct tells me it has something to do with the memory of not succeeding the first time. For the same reason, prospective lawyers who do not pass the Bar exam the first time have a receding rate of passage each subsequent time they take it. I say this so you appreciate how rare it is to be afforded an opportunity to re-negotiate.

So how do you approach things? Each situation, depending on the underlying facts and circumstances, will require an assessment. For example, sometimes a hard 'no' may mean 'maybe' if you try again the next day or soften your stance. I recently purchased a car from a local dealership. After driving the car, my wife and I loved it. It was also within our price range. When I made an offer, the manager expressed a willingness to only drop the price by $250. Accepting would still keep me within my budget, but the hard-line approach was unpalatable to me. Further, I had a good reason to believe the car wouldn't be sold within the next 24 hours, given the existence of a buyers-market. The dealer, strengthening my conviction, had acknowledged that the vehicle in which I was interested had been listed for a long time. In other words, they were eager to sell it.

At the same time, I liked the car, felt it was a good deal, and was anxious to move forward. I was prepared to show up the next afternoon and accept, at that time, their final offer. In the interim, I was hoping they would re-open the negotiations by calling me. I was lucky when they did call the next morning. The associate who called me came short of accepting my final offer, but the mere fact of his calling to "talk things over" set up a nice opportunity for me to re-position myself. I asked him to drop it $250 more, a compromise from my last offer of $500 less than his best figure. It worked, and a deal was consummated.

In my car-purchasing example, many things went well. For one, I was fortunate that the dealership called, an event over which I had no control. I also created an environment in which a subsequent deal could happen. I left the initial meeting on good terms. By re-initiating communication and understanding the market, I felt there was a chance of success. Again, I won't minimize the role luck played.

In some situations, waiting a longer time is advisable. Consider this hypothetical: Your home purchase negotiations have broken down. During the subsequent several months, you attend numerous open houses and review listings periodically. Nothing, however, draws your interest. The housing market's soft, and the home you liked remains listed, perhaps even at a lower price. Assuming the talks broke down amicably, the additional time will serve you well in re-opening discussions.

Another example of the benefit of waiting is the concept of 'outlasting' your opponent. If you're dealing with a corporation, there's always a chance your contact person will be fired, laid off, or will quit in the period following the breakdown in your negotiations. If so, his or her replacement may have a more accommodating personality or more decision-making freedom. You may be surprised at how easy it is to negotiate a deal with the new person. Comparably, the corporation could dissolve or sell to a different entity.

In my work as a trial lawyer, the concepts of 'outlasting' and 'waiting' are prominent. Consider that the average lifetime of a case in the court system (a.k.a. litigation) is about two years.

If you're dealing with a medium or large firm on the other side, statistically, it's probable during that time an associate will leave the firm, perhaps be promoted to partner, or be removed from the case. Other possibilities include that a different judge will be assigned to the case, the opposing law firm will be fired by its client, or that financial circumstances or life events will change for either party such that a negotiated settlement becomes more or less likely.

Using the example of litigation, say your opponent has tendered an initial offer of $5,000 to settle a collections case in which you claim he owes $20,000. He may be "low balling" you in the hope you accept with an eagerness of avoiding the expenses and uncertainties of protracted litigation. By slowing down the process and waiting, you may cause your opponent to incur high legal fees. It may therefore catalyze the settlement process.

Finally, I think it is appropriate to finish this chapter with a common theme. Whether engaged in negotiations at an initial session or reopening discussions months or even years later, be mindful of appearing desperate. Remember, we all want to make advantageous deals. Getting to that point requires finesse and detachment. Don't be too eager when re-negotiating because your opponent may sense your eagerness and desperation and know he can get a better deal by saying no or waiting. At that point, you have only two choices, neither of which is attractive: You can accept the terms being dictated by your opponent if you are in fact desperate or you can wait. With both options, you are not obtaining your objective, namely a good deal.

Approach the re-institution of negotiations with the 'can't lose' spirit, which should characterize your approach to this entire process.

K. The Broken Deal

Say you have successfully negotiated the purchase of a car or been fortunate in re-negotiating the sale of a home. You have done the hard part, but there's more. In certain situations, the agreement may not last over time. In such cases, you will have to choose between re-negotiating and walking away.

In addressing the preliminary question of why deals break down, let us work in an example. You're a small-time landlord. By this, I mean either you rent out an apartment in a multi-family house or you rent out less than three apartments in other buildings. Assume the rental market is favorable for tenants. Interest rates are low, prompting people to buy real estate instead of renting. As a landlord, this leaves you in a vulnerable spot.

Let's add another unfavorable fact: You have a sophisticated, opportunistic, and slightly immoral tenant who capitalizes on these trends while he is under a lease with you. Perhaps he notices comparable apartments which are priced lower than the one for which he has contracted with you. So, he tells you he will break his lease and move out unless you lower the rent.

You have no legal obligation to concede to his pressure. From a practical standpoint, though, if he leaves and you sue him you may spend money in legal fees to collect against someone who is relatively judgment-proof (meaning that the tenant has no assets or money to satisfy a judgment). For Self-Righteous Landlords ("SRL's"), the loaded concept of justice may take over. On principal, they'll refuse to re-negotiate with their opportunistic tenants. It is unfair, they'll say. The lease lasts a year and if they break it there are consequences, they'll add. The SRLs contend they have lawyers in waiting who'll sue these bastards until right is done and the dead-beat tenants are taught a powerful lesson.

Don't be an SRL or behave like one. From a practical standpoint, SRLs will pay considerably more in legal fees than they will lose in income by agreeing to a lower rent. This cost neither considers the likelihood of obtaining an uncollectible judgment or the amount of time and energy (not to mention ill feelings) you will invest in the process of retribution. Money is money, and as a landlord, you are in the business of maximizing profits. Don't make it personal; getting distracted by self-righteousness can be hazardous.

Let's return to our example with the opportunistic tenant. Once you let go of your obstructing sense of vulnerability, take a comfortable breath, because the next step is tougher: You'll need to be proactive in contacting your tenant. Remember, luck is not with you at the moment. Further, though life is good, it is not always fair. The rental market is bad. Even if you could replace your tenant, you likely would have to settle on a lower rent. In addition, there is always cost in replacing tenants (e.g. book-keeping, repairs, etc.). In short, your best financial choice would be to keep your current tenant at a lower rent.

How do you approach the re-negotiation? With reluctance, I am forced to again give a lawyerly answer and say it somewhat depends on the circumstances and the person with whom you are negotiating. That said, here are my guidelines, using the example of the opportunistic tenant: First, don't immediately respond to his or her request for a lower rent. Let him/her think about and worry over your potential responses.

Then spend a few days analyzing the rental market to confirm or refute your tenant's suggestion. Assuming he is correct and the market is sluggish, I would respond in writing to your tenant, saying you've reviewed his request and wish to meet to discuss the issue. Avoid any negative or self-pitying comments or innuendos (e.g. "Just my luck that rentals have taken a nose dive"). Keep it simple, professional and business-like. Emotions have no place in this equation. (I've repeated these words, but that's intentional). I would also suggest some dates and times when you are available to meet at your tenant's home. Remember, you want to make the meeting as non-threatening and accommodating to your tenant as possible. Also, don't shift to the other extreme by endorsing your tenant's opportunistic and manipulative ways. Focus on the fact that you are choosing the best available business option.

Having sanitized any residual feelings of self-righteousness, you are ready for the next step: the meeting with your tenant. Request that he propose what he thinks is a reasonable rent. Keep in mind that while he may be in the better negotiating position, he would prefer to make a deal to stay. Moving is expensive, as well as irritating. Some of the housekeeping tasks involved are: paying movers, paying the new landlord first months rent and security deposit, switching phone and utility bills to the new address, and decorating the new place. These chores are magnified if your opportunistic tenant hasn't yet found a suitable new apartment.

You should be able to determine if your tenant's demand is reasonable based on your independent research. If it is not, you should share your data and sources with your tenant, in the hope that he becomes logical. Be mindful of your tone and of keeping your emotions in check. If your tenant acts with belligerence, threats, or stubbornness, you'll know that no deal can be reached. With gentleness, remind him that you are not obligated to re-negotiate, that he would be breaking the lease by leaving prematurely, and that you reserve all rights in that regard. To take any other posture would, most if not all of the time, cast a fatal spell on your negotiations. Walk out on the same terms under which you entered. If he responds with immaturity or heightened threats, smile if you wish, but don't be goaded into saying or doing anything purely for ego purposes. Hasten to the door.

Alternatively, your tenant may be reasonable and throw a number at you, which may only be a couple of hundred dollars less than what he currently pays. If you feel the meeting is productive, but not definitive in resolving the issue, listen to your instincts. Maybe arranging a second in-person meeting would be advantageous. It might make sense to continue your negotiations by phone.

In the rare case your opportunistic tenant plays the sympathy card (e.g. "Times are tough for me") don't dismiss him, but be careful to avoid his emotional trap. Remember, he was the one who contacted you about lowering his rent, reflecting his awareness of the current market trend. Guard the dispassionate middle ground vital to successful business negotiations. Say a word to comfort him, such as, "It must be tough to lose your job. I'm sorry to hear that." But don't go beyond those statements. Hopefully, the conversation will then return to the main line, namely determining fair rent.

Assuming the initial meeting goes well, the follow-up should be easy. Make sure you memorialize your agreement in writing. That way, there will be no future misunderstandings. In exchange for your willingness to lower the rent, see if your tenant will agree to extend the term of the lease. For example, if the written lease ends in five months, try to extend it for eight or nine months at the lower rate or have a graduated rent that increases toward the end of the term.

In this chapter, I've exclusively used the example of a residential lease to elucidate what I believe are the essential issues in re-negotiation. It's worth emphasizing, though, that negotiating or re-negotiating leases are unique in that there is an ongoing relationship between a landlord and a tenant. That is clearly not the case in all negotiations (e.g. home or car purchases). Your re-negotiation strategy will therefore depend on the circumstances and the subject matter involved.

L. Finalizing the Deal

You don't need to be a lawyer to appreciate the value of written contracts. If a dispute occurs between two parties and their understanding is oral, obvious interpretation problems can arise. The potential trouble spots compound where the agreement is specific.

PART I

Let's take the example of hiring a contractor. I haven't always had the best experiences with plumbers, electricians, painters, etc. I suppose the same concept applies to police officers, lawyers and doctors in that some in those fields are professional and competent while others make your neck hairs bristle. Nonetheless, I find that informality reigns in the home contracting field. Schedules and appointments, I say with sarcasm and truth, are optional to the contractor.

If you own a two-bedroom condominium and hire a flooring guy to replace your carpeting with wood, make sure your agreement is reduced to writing before making a down payment. I speak from experience. Once I hired a wood flooring specialist for such a project, and I negotiated what I thought was a fair price. I failed to insist on a written agreement, as doing so often invites suspicion, uneasiness, and administrative hassle. Then, I paid for half of the cost, agreeing to pay the balance upon completion.

Two days later, after taking a second look at my unit, the contractor announced a problem. Since there was concrete under the carpeting, he would need to first set a layer of plywood. The cost would grow by fifty percent. Fifty percent! So, I stepped back, trying to keep my composure. I reminded him, as I had learned in law school, that we had a contract even thought it was oral. Its terms were simple: He would do the flooring work and I would pay him the agreed upon fee, in two installments. He claimed that had he known the underlying floor was cement, he never would have agreed to the low price.

Had I committed him to a written contract, I believe he would have been forced to do the extra work at the original price. My problem was worsened by the fact that I had already tendered a down payment, meaning it would have been more difficult to walk from the deal.

The first point in finalizing the deal is a simple one: Reduce your understanding to writing. The obvious benefit is illustrated in my flooring example. The detractors will stress the most

41

popular reason why people fail to do so, namely because writings can prove cumbersome. This deterrence becomes heightened with more complicated written agreements. The naysayers, who profess to be experts but ironically have limited negotiating experience, may bark about how writings delay negotiations. My response is that a quick negotiating session may yield an even quicker verbal agreement. If that deal breaks down, because of the potential for misunderstandings and multiple interpretations which characterize such arrangements, you have nothing.

As the cliché goes, "A verbal agreement is only as good as the paper it's written on."

That said, the naysayers' dissention is not without merit. Having an agreement is my recommendation, but be sure that the agreement isn't fifteen pages. I'm exaggerating, but you get my point. Patient and reasonable people will grow frustrated if you over-do a written proposal. Lawyers have a reputation for wordiness, but I've noticed this trait in many non-lawyers when they draft legal documents. Perhaps our society has falsely led them to believe that confusing, incomprehensible sentences are the essence of legal documents. If so, they are disillusioned.

How long should an agreement be? Well, I would advise you to focus on content instead of length. The question, rephrased, becomes: What should a negotiated agreement consist of? At the risk of annoying you, I'm afraid I must again qualify the question with my disclaimer that I offer general rules. The facts and circumstances of each negotiation must be considered in order to tailor the content of your written agreement.

Since agreements either involve the sale of goods or services or concern leasing, price is an important issue and must be highlighted in the written agreement. Other necessities include the services to be provided and the period under which the services are to be performed or the manner in which the goods are to be produced or delivered.

PART I

Consider these items as well: warranties, insurance, defining consequences if one party breaches, and contact information. It also helps to add specifics based on the type of transaction. When dealing with contractors, make sure their licensure information appears in the agreement. That way, if there are workmanship issues, you will have recourse with the local licensing board. In some instances, there may be criminal consequences if a contractor has failed to secure a certain license or pulled the requisite permits.

Massachusetts and some other states have set up consumer agencies which specifically handle complaints against contractors. The advantages of proceeding in this fashion, versus trying your hand in the court system, are clear. For one, the consumer agencies set up a speedy hearing, whereas litigation may take years before a trial date is obtained. Cost is also a benefit. The agencies, as their name suggests, are much more consumer-friendly than are the courts. This means that in addition to saving money on filing fees, you will avoid exorbitant legal fees. (I'm anticipating an unfriendly reaction from some of my lawyer colleagues who thrive on bilking clients). The key point with most of these agencies is that they require the contractor's licensing information. For those that do not, your chances of prevailing at the hearing, thereby proving your case, are enhanced when you have a written contract.

A common question may be: How do I raise my desire for a written contract if the person with whom I am negotiating appears resistant to the idea? If the person is refusing the request outright, you have no viable option but to walk from the deal. Their outright refusal should signal an immediate red flag that they may be a shady businessperson. If there is no summary refusal, I would say something like the following: "My preference is to put everything in writing; that way there won't be any genuine misunderstandings…I'd be happy to put something together." An important thing to note: Because of what is known as the Parol Evidence Rule, you are bound to the "four corners of your written document" which means that no prior oral agreements will be considered. Only the terms of your written, signed agreement are considered valid. Of course, as with every law concept, there are exceptions, but strict compliance with this rule will prove to be highly beneficial to you.

Often the person with whom you are negotiating will offer to prepare the contract or may have a prepared form that he presents to you. Never sign immediately upon presentation. Carefully review each word. If anything does not make sense, ask for an explanation. If what he or she says sounds different from what appears in the agreement, voice your desire to re-word that particular provision of the agreement.

Don't shy from adding items which are absent from the contract. Remember that once you have signed it, there's no ability to change anything without the other side's consent. Therefore, make sure you are comfortable with the final draft prior to executing it.

Make sure you obtain a copy of the executed agreement. If not, you will encounter difficulty proving that you had one.

Once you have a clear, simple agreement, the chance of problems occurring diminishes.

How would the naysayers respond to that?

M. Post Deal Niceties

Once you've cemented the deal you're done, right? Time to move to the next task, you may think. Why devote a section to something that bears nothing on the deal you've already consummated?

I'm forced to revisit and confront a demon that presented itself in *Unlearning Law School*, namely a canard that flows as follows: "Nice guys finish last." Its proponents flout half-truths in support of their theory (flawed for reasons we'll get to in a moment) that kindness equals business doom. In *Unlearning Law School*, I attacked these naysayers by noting that folks prefer dealing with people they like. Further, people like those who are nice to them. It reasons, then, that being nice will lead to more business.

What does this have to do with post-deal niceties? Simple. Your vision in negotiations must be long-term and all-inclusive, not myopic. Others may disagree but my fervent and time-tested belief is that kindness works. To that end, I accentuate the person when I complete the deal. By personalizing the process, your opponent will realize that you're not such a bad guy. He'll feel good, if he doesn't already, about the deal and be eager to do business with you in the future. One of my all-time favorite negotiators was the late Red Auerbach, former head coach of those great Boston Celtics basketball teams of the 1950's and 60's. Auerbach was reputed as a shrewd but harsh negotiator who would use the media and any other available means to undercut a player seeking what he felt was an unreasonable contract. Nonetheless, he was equally famous for the ready and aggressive fashion with which he repaired ill-feeling once a deal was reached.

How? I like letters, both giving and receiving them. A few years ago, I bought a car from a dealership and the salesman's demeanor was a factor in my decision to buy there. Two days after purchasing the car I received a concise letter from him. In it, he thanked me for my business and assured me he would respond to any future concerns on this car or any car I bought from him. There was nothing phony or gimmicky about it. It likely took him only a few minutes to put it together. I know the letter was sent to promote his business. That's OK. The fact is he wants my business, in a professional way, and that makes me eager to work with him.

Why do so many business people either fail to express appreciation after a deal is consummated or show it in a way that is fluffy and contrived? Consider how you would feel if in contrast to the letter I received from the car salesman, you received something like this:

> *"Dear Joe,*
>
> *Glad you made Happy Chevrolet your partner! With a winning attitude, a staff that never quits, and over 10,000 vehicles sold, we care about only 1 thing: our customers! We love our customers! That's right. Happy Chevrolet didn't get its name for nothing!"*

Makes you want to vomit, doesn't it? One wonders if the brass at Happy Chevrolet would enjoy receiving that same sleazy form letter. Probably not. To answer the earlier question posed, I think business people fail to show sincere appreciation either because they don't value its importance or because they lack the requisite people skills to successfully touch others.

If you're not a letter-writer, a phone call can suffice. The key is to do it without strings. Call because you want to express thanks or that you appreciated working with the other person or whatever other nicety you have in mind. It feels good when someone calls just because they want to say 'hi' without an agenda.

Keep in mind the long-term and ongoing nature of negotiations. They may not be specific to the deal you have completed. Nonetheless, you may be in business yourself and may receive future business from the person with whom you have been dealing.

Why not say a few words to ingratiate them?

Alternatively, the person with whom you are negotiating may have been referred by a friend or acquaintance. An amicable departing would almost certainly find its way back to your friend, thereby bolstering your reputation as a kind-hearted person.

So, why not say a few words to ingratiate them?

N. Dealing with Difficult People—Select Case Studies

Success in negotiations and generally in life hinges on your ability to 'deal' with (for lack of a better phrase) people you don't like. The operative word here is 'deal', so I've put it in quotations. You don't need to socialize with these types nor do you need to befriend them. Were that the case, depression and other mental illnesses could inflict you.

This discussion, more so than any other part of the book, has undergone considerable revision and supplementation. Why is that? The answer is simple yet sad: our society abounds with toxic types. Whenever I thought I had completed this section satisfactorily, a new encounter with a mentally-challenged person would take hold and require insertion. A quick and humorous example comes to mind: I represented this disabled man who is the beneficiary of a special needs trust. That means the trustee of the trustee is responsible for dispersing monies for his expenses and personal welfare. The problem is that the trustee is an older lawyer whose disrespect for my client (the beneficiary) is only exceeded by his own arrogance and sense of entitlement. I've written to and spoken with the self-important trustee (SIT) several times in an effort to secure reimbursement for the beneficiary's expenses and to increase his stipend. The SIT (ironic given his laziness) rebuffs my attempts, his responses laced with snide and self-aggrandizing remarks (e.g. referencing my foolish youth, his important writings and his other more significant cases). How dare I question his work as trustee, he fumed. My client and I should count ourselves lucky to have a person of his stature as trustee. Further, he talks over me, rarely listening or respecting my viewpoint. He characterized a letter I had written as 'defamatory' (quite a charge) but was unable to cite any defamatory statement in it – per my request. In a subsequent conversation, he instructed me not to call for two weeks and hung up the phone on me after rambling about some 'important' work he had to do. I laughed to myself upon reflection.

So how do you handle someone like the SIT? Not an easy question to answer, even for someone like me who writes on that subject. The truth is, these are difficult people with whom to deal. They try to sap your energy, push you around, and weave you into their twisted agendas. Be patient with yourself.

To begin: Why do you need to deal with them and what does that mean? I'm assuming that these toxic types are active participants in the scenario you are negotiating. If not, of course, you would not need to engage them. If so, to answer the first question, they are essential to your successful resolution of the matter. To ignore them would be fatal to the negotiating process.

What dealing with toxic people entails may vary from person to person, making the crafting of a definition challenging. The following suggestions might be helpful as you navigate in this arena. Sarcasm and humor, while necessary releases in many circumstances, are dangerous instruments in dealing with toxic people. Why is that? What follows is my layperson's assessment, to be distinguished from the opinions and diagnoses of a licensed medical professional. Unhappy people are typically insecure about themselves due to the unkind acts of others at some juncture of their earlier life. Maybe it was the fifth grade bully who embarrassed them in front of others or perhaps it was a critical or abusive parent. It follows that they often don't find humor in the same things that you or I would. This is especially true if you attempt self-deprecating humor (as they may take a serious stab at you) or if you gently rib them (as they may react with anger and retaliation). In short, their world is so askew that they cannot appreciate your humor. It is therefore pointless, so don't even try it. Laughing or smiling at his humor attempts, however, will likely soothe his ego.

The second general rule is to resist sharing your innermost thoughts. A critic of this view would chirp how I'm encouraging emotional dishonesty. I am, but in the limited context of dealing with difficult people, which represents a small percentage of

PART I

your time. Why should you tell these people exactly how you feel? They won't be supportive. In fact, if you share something personal, they might twist the facts and then blab it to their fellow misanthropes.

Here's a final nugget of advice: Use humor and empathy to your advantage in dealing with these troubled souls. Remember what I suggested earlier, that toxic people project the lack of love which they feel and the pain which accompanies it. It's sad when considered in that regard. Picture the forty-year-old angry person with whom you're dealing today as a scrawny seven-year-old with glasses. Imagine further that he and the rest of his class are picking sides for a kickball game. The two team captains take turns choosing players, and the first captain says, "Looks like four-eyes is last again." The other piles on the verbal abuse, adding, "Yeah, we don't want stickman on our team. He sucks." Then a third boy pushes him in the back and he stumbles, dropping his glasses. More laughter. More teasing. The words may sound innocuous to an adult, but they sting a child.

The boy walks home with his head down that evening. He lives alone with his mother, who has too many problems of her own to pay much regard to his suffering, so his issues, fears, and insecurities are dismissed, minimized or exacerbated when he is blamed for his weakness.

As the boy ages, his work ethic and book smarts earn him some success in school and the business world, but he remains insecure and emotionally-traumatized by the bullying he experienced in his youth. What you are encountering, then, is an adult version of that seven-year-old who now resorts to the tactics of which he was a victim. His behavior is therefore cyclical and pathetic.

Find some humor in the conduct of this social idiot. Do not laugh in his face, but do laugh to yourself. Remind yourself that most people in the world are good and decent. None of us is anywhere near perfect, but perfection and semi-normal behavior are different animals. It follows that most people, if allowed to witness the deranged behavior of this strange person, would validate your feelings. In other words, his conduct may irritate, frustrate, and even upset you, but he is not targeting you.

It is tough, in my view, to make sense of the fact that he/she is the problem, not you. On paper, the rationale is perfect. Why then, is it so challenging to grasp when it plays out in your real life? In a nutshell, I feel we are all sensitive to criticism and people expressing disapproval toward us. It hurts when we are not liked, and it is tough to recalibrate that mindset.

<u>Toxic People: Examples</u>

1. The Word Twister ("WT")

You might also think of this devilish character as the t'is/t'aint person. That is, if you say t'is, he or she will say t'aint. WTs delight in your discomfort and strive to make you question what you have actually said. A WT is self-righteous, condescending and, above all, pugnacious.

The sad reality, to which I have alluded both in this book and in *Unlearning Law School*, is that lawyers seem predisposed to these bad behaviors. I am sure it has something to do with our work as advocates and the nature of an adversarial system. But, I do not like to use that reason as an excuse. By analogy, some karate black belts abuse their special talent by threatening others, instead of exercising the restraint which such access to power mandates.

In acting as your own lawyer it is likely you will, at some point, encounter the WT. I remember several years ago encountering an opposing lawyer in a divorce case who had practiced longer than I, and this pompous loser knew it and expected to wrap it around me as if I were some Christmas present. From the moment I met him at an initial court hearing and he spurned my extended hand, I sensed the type of person with whom I was dealing.

On subsequent occasions, he would roll his eyes at things I

would say during meetings and make constant reference to how he perceived my lack of experience as his certain victory. I remember one time he claimed I was "in over my head". Ironically, my client and I succeeded in the initial hearings. Whenever I reminded him of this particular fact, he would again roll his eyes, smile in an awkward way, or do one of those patronizing and phony laughs that make the reasonable man sick to his stomach. Then he would twist the truth, spinning the facts so as to make it appear that his failings were actually part of his larger strategy and that I had gained nothing from those triumphs. Further, he would misrepresent the context of our conversations to the court.

How do you deal with the WT and his litany of psychological babble? At one time I subscribed to the famous childhood adage that "Sticks and stones may break my bones, but names will never hurt me..." Sometimes that approach works, particularly where the WT is powerless by isolating himself from others. More often, I have learned, silence is a dangerous response.

I am not suggesting you spend considerable emotional or financial resources in a fruitless quest to straighten out the insidious conduct of the WT. That would not be wise. It would also be useless to attempt reconciliation with the WT. It would be prudent, however, to make a brief and pointed response to the WT's attacks.

How one should respond must be dictated by the particular circumstances at hand. There are some basic guidelines, applicable to most cases. First, keep your emotions out of it. If you sense yourself becoming angry, that is not the time to respond. To the extent the circumstances permit, I would recommend your response/rebuttal/correction of inaccurate information be presented to a neutral third party. When a case is in court, this process of rebuttal is easy. Simply provide the judge with the accurate information orally or in writing. Where the case is not in court and there are no neutrals to whom you can appeal, you must respond to WT. Make sure you do so in writing to keep an adequate paper trial.

My second general suggestion is that after you put out the fire the WT has created, resist a counter-attack, unless it is strategically necessary. In other words, do not mimic the WT's conduct. You likely will not need to. Furthermore, doing so will deplete your energy.

2. Two-Faced Sleaze ("TFS")

My experiences with certain TFS' have changed an opinion I once maintained that I could make an immediate judgment on a person. I used to think those initial fifteen minutes or so of conversation would suffice in drawing a character determination. Many times it works. High integrity or a scoundrel's ways are revealed.

Occasionally, though, such is not the case. The TFS plays (and preys) on his belief that he can win your trust initially, only to exploit this vulnerability at a later point.

My recent encounter and subsequent dealings with a TFS insurance defense lawyer will hopefully illustrate my points. Essentially, he needed to secure the deposition testimony of my clients, non-parties, to assist his defense in the underlying case. I do not want to get into specifics beyond that, so as to protect the confidentiality of the clients given the publicity that the case received.

So this insurance lawyer called me and, in gentle terms, explained how his client and mine were the victims of this third party who had brought suit against his client. To paraphrase his shtick: "You're a good guy; I'm a good guy; Let's work together to make this as easy for our perspective clients as possible by cooperating and collaborating." Most people, like me, would feel comfortable with that proposal. I knew nothing of the guy, so I had no reason to harbor skepticism of his motive. Plus, optimism runs at my core. I want to believe and trust people.

At the informal meeting he arranged with my clients and me, he asked them a series of questions, made small talk about his early days as a struggling lawyer, and expressed empathy for their plight. In subsequent private conversations, he assured me that his client would work with mine to protect their mutual interests.

Then, this TFS insurance lawyer unloaded the litigation version of Pearl Harbor on me. He filed motions, in several of the courts in which his cases were pending, to add my clients as liable parties! To exacerbate matters, he alleged my client had engaged in a conspiracy with the party that had sued the insurance company—to commit insurance fraud. But, it was worse than that! He alleged untrue and twisted facts based on my clients' representations at the informal meeting we voluntarily attended.

What do you do when a TFS has violated your trust to that degree? Don't blame yourself or question your decision to take an optimistic posture. To do so would squander opportunities to meet interesting people, make new friends, and conduct effective business. As soon as you identify the antics of a TFS, though, cut off contact to the extent you are able. In my case, there was no more opportunity to negotiate. As far as I was concerned, he had declared war against my clients and me. I gave peace a chance, and he could no longer be trusted.

I filed an opposition to his motion, attacking his conduct and illuminating it to the court. When competing against someone unscrupulous, it is important to control your instinct to mimic his behavior. At the same time, avoiding the necessary confrontation and failing to rectify the TFS' factual inaccuracies promises an exacerbation of the problem.

Chances are good, as was the case with my TFS, that your nightmare will protest your response. He will say or write something like, "What are you doing? Why are you making this so difficult", as if his one wish were to befriend you. In so doing, he will manipulate so as to portray you as the aggressor. That is why you need to keep your distance, limiting your verbal communications to terse written responses when necessary. The key is to reject his nonsense without qualifying or questioning your instincts.

When you make it clear to him that you are done dealing with him, a strange phenomenon will take hold. This folksy, gregarious person will transform to a man-child (or woman-child, as the case may be). What do I mean by that? Let me illustrate by using the above example. When I presented my TFS' trail of lies, material omissions, and pattern of unethical behavior, he erupted in open court. He confronted me with veiled threats in the hallway following the hearing. He suggested I had better watch myself- "for my own good". Give me a break. Did he really care about me? I walked away during his meltdown.

I think what a TFS wants is attention and the subjugation of your ego to his. Remember, your TFS is a wounded child who is crying out for approval. As you know, children will pout and throw tantrums to get what they want. Don't get suckered. A TFS is poison wrapped in sugar. He has no regard for your welfare or the integrity which is so requisite to deal making. Sadly, though, he is equally disrespectful to himself, likely feeling so low, ineffectual, and insecure that he needs to project these nasty thoughts onto you and me.

Don't give him the chance. Keep him at a distance, protecting yourself by reducing necessary communications to writing.

3. The Silent Back-Stabber ("SBS")

I suppose the good thing about the TFS is, if you keep your eyes open, you'll soon begin to see him unravel. In some instances, you'd have to be blind or oblivious in failing to witness his outrageous conduct. He's often a yeller and a screamer, and when pushed, will arm you with sufficient verbal ammunition to take him down.

The same cannot be said for the SBS. That's what makes him so difficult. Most of the time you've got a moving target. He'll simply 'yes' you, smiling and accommodating everything you say. Then he or she will indirectly, through something said

PART I

to a third party, attempt to sabotage you.

Here's my best personal experience with an SBS. My second legal job after graduating law school was in a small personal injury firm in Springfield, Massachusetts. The sole partner was greed-driven and rarely available, often leaving the rest of us to our own devices. In any event, after I began, the firm hired another young lawyer whose air of haughtiness was apparent from the day she started.

Nonetheless, my mantra is always to seek peace over war, so I made an effort to be polite, even deferential to her on occasion. For example, I helped her out on cases she was handling and kept quiet when certain secretaries and paralegals began to verbalize their concerns about her scheming ways.

Slowly, I began to sense she was badmouthing me, complaining about the quality of my work to supervisors and saying unkind things about me as a person. I could not, at the time, confirm these suspicions, though they were palpable. I took what I felt was the higher road, namely giving her the full benefit of my many doubts by continuing to be cordial. Peace feels better than war and, in my view, the latter policy should only be pursued when there is irrefutable proof.

Days later I would receive such proof. Two of my close friends in the office, who were secretaries, shared a revolting story about this SBS. They said she told them I was a "Lazy Jew" and that she was doing most of my work for me. The latter accusation, though patently untrue, was at least moderately tolerable. The first part was a declaration of war.

I will not mince words in saying I fumed upon hearing this recounting. My instinct and adrenaline drove me to consider an immediate confrontation. But as my anger simmered, I wondered what that would accomplish. She'd deny the allegation. I'd have to reveal my sources. Further, she'd likely continue to bash me.

A better idea came to mind, and I put it to the test the next morning when I saw her in the office. I greeted her and requested a moment alone with her, which she obliged. I said, "One of the girls told me you said something which I know could not be true."

Her eyes perked.

Then I told her what I heard, again emphasizing how I believed her over them. My objective was to avoid appearing confrontational and accusatory. If I did that, I felt it would be easy for her to deny and point back at me as falsely attacking her. In other words, I'd allow her to escape by playing her 'pity' card.

When I repeated the vile comments for her, her response lacked the shock one would expect of a falsely-accused person. I read her eyes to suggest she seemed more surprised I had discovered her mean comments or, perhaps more appropriately, that someone had revealed her.

She was still and silent for five seconds, before she said, "Of course I would never say anything like that." The detachment in her words was chilling.

So, I spread it thicker, saying "I knew it. I knew you would never say anything like that."

Now maybe I'm wrong here, but if someone falsely accused me of pronouncing such incendiary, anti-Semitic comments, I'd demand to know who my defamer was. She stayed silent, though, after she had spoken her piece. My initial instincts as to her culpability were cemented.

I'm sure she thought I was crazy but, as anticipated, she was subsequently deferential with me. She seemed nervous whenever I entered the room. There may be people who feel a more direct confrontation would work better. Perhaps, but keep in mind the circumstances.

If your SBS, as was the case with mine, is someone with whom you will have regular dealings, I would advise against blunt confrontation. Subtlety and finesse, in my view, are more effective weapons in your arsenal.

Whatever you do (and this advice would apply to all toxic

people), don't blame yourself or try to fix these warped individuals. Negotiating effectively with toxic types tests your patience and ability to implement winning strategies.

PART II

PURSUING CLAIMS & UNDERSTANDING RIGHTS

Some sad souls cling to the depressing belief that the world is out to get them. We've talked a bit about them already. They bark out generalities like "You can't trust anyone" and "Everyone's out for him or herself." At the other extreme are the idealists who pretend that everyone, particularly those in positions of power, are devoted servants of the public welfare. Most people, of course, fit somewhere between these polarized philosophies.

My feelings on the matter draw from both extremes. On the one hand, I consider myself an optimist. I believe most people and corporations are honest and law-abiding. Corporate scams draw headlines. They bear similarities to the isolated incidents of police brutality, priest misconduct, or medical malpractice. In other words, though the media often thrives on exaggeration and interesting stories, reality is different.

That said, on the rare occasion when you encounter someone with 'dirty hands,' I differ from my idealistic friends who either enable bad behavior by pretending it doesn't exist or by ignoring it when they see it happen. Here is the essence of my view on the matter: I do not seek confrontation, but when no other alternative appears, one needs to confront whomever or whatever is involved in the so-called claim. To do otherwise would undermine your Due Process rights as an American. Further, how can you feel good about yourself if you are always conceding in the name of peace?

You do not need a law degree to advocate for yourself.

A. Clerical Matters

My wife, older son, and I formerly lived in Boston, where parking is an issue. We had to pay careful attention to signs that spoke to street cleaning days, resident permit issues, metering, etc. To raise revenue, I believe our government capitalizes on nuanced and often antiquated parking laws which don't make much sense. For example, you can get a ticket if you are not parked a certain distance from the curb or from a fire hydrant. If you double-park in front of your apartment or condo building, you may get ticketed. Our meter maids have been known to hide in areas where double parkers are prominent. On one occasion, I saw a meter maid measuring the distance between the wheel of a parked car and the curb, hoping for a violation of the pertinent city ordinance. Perhaps he was vying for 'employee of the month' by serving the most tickets.

I can see getting a ticket for parking in a handicapped spot or being too close to a fire hydrant, maybe even for double-parking longer than a reasonable time. But using a measuring stick to play 'gotcha'? That brings to mind an example of outrageous meter-maid conduct. A few Thanksgivings ago, my parents came over to our condo in the city for dinner. My mother pulled her car up in front of our building to unload the food she had prepared. With the hazard blinkers on, I helped her carry several heavy items into the house. When I returned to the car, having left it unattended a maximum of two minutes, I saw a meter maid writing out a ticket. There was simply no other reasonable choice but to double-park her car. We could have parked it in a lot half a mile away and carried the heavy food, though that wasn't practical.

PART II

I believe I did what most would do: Appealing to her purported sense of decency, I made my case. But she was implacable, insisting that once she began the ticket-writing process, she was obligated to stick us. "How could you do so under these circumstances?" I pleaded. After all, we were gone for only a matter of minutes. Thanksgiving? Holiday spirit? Common sense? My mother visiting? Decency? Don't those simple concepts mean anything? Apparently not to this "friendly" meter maid.

To cut the story down, I appealed the $30 or $40 ticket and prevailed. I can't speak for other jurisdictions, but in Boston most people don't bother appealing parking tickets. The success rate on appeals, though, is quite high. With speeding tickets, the appeal process is even more favorable. You are afforded a hearing before a clerk magistrate. Even if you lose that hearing, you get a new one before a judge. Here's the key point: If the officer that cited you does not show for the second hearing, the case must get dismissed.

When you have a legitimate gripe, you don't need a lawyer to knock off a parking or speeding ticket. With the latter, a successful appeal will not only save you the $100 or $150 ticket, it will prevent your insurance premium from jumping. Even if you admit to a mistake at the hearing, the clerk may let you off on a warning if you stress your good driving record, citizenship, etc. In any event, it's worth a try.

What other clerical matters are we talking about? In the private sector, this includes such tasks as disputing cable, utility, and telephone bills. The advantage to the consumer in seeking recompense or redress from one of those large corporations is that you can easily climb the employee hierarchy if necessary.

For example, say you were over-charged on a cable bill. Initially you'll be set up with a low-level employee whose role is likely to comfort dissatisfied customers. These folks are programmed to spew out niceties that make it sound as if their company is in the hospitality business. He or she usually lacks the authority to enter the appropriate credit or rebate, so he'll express empathy (real or phony) for your concern and try to explain away your dispute. Most people will let it go at that point and pay the extra amount on the bill. Resist that temptation.

Instead, emphasize to him that you enjoy the company's cable service. If you have used them for a number of years and have paid all bills on time, make mention of that fact. If he refuses to act, then you will need to speak to his supervisor. Keep your tone controlled and professional. If you are too demanding or antagonistic, even if justified on the merits, you will undercut your goal.

In my experience, the supervisor will relent and either accommodate your specific request or forge a compromise offer. On the rare occasion that the supervisor is either unwilling or unable to be flexible or where you are unwilling to accept his offer, you have a choice. Option number one is to relinquish your demand. That is probably not going to feel great. The other option is to terminate your account or, in the case of a disputed bill, be prepared to face the unappealing prospect of collection proceedings. If you feel strongly in your opposition, do not worry (as some unfortunately do) that your good credit will be ruined. If they do report the alleged debt to a credit bureau, it should be noted as just an "alleged debt". Be sure you can contact one of the major credit bureaus and let them know that you dispute the debt claim. Concern in this regard should not deter you from pursuing or defending a discrepancy which you believe should be rectified.

I should modify the general rule on such disputes, with regard to credit reporting, with a brief discussion on IRS claims. I don't know about you, but the phrase 'IRS claims' puts me in a bad space when I'm feeling good, and when I'm in a low mood it can cause heart palpitations. The reason is that, either real or imagined, the IRS wields more power than do private entities. Therefore, if you are disputing an IRS claim, which I once did on behalf of my wife, make sure you do so in the

PART II

formal fashion they require. In the case of my wife, they were claiming back taxes were owed based on a mistake made by her former employer. We provided the correct written documentation, and they dismissed the claim.

The respectable concept of standing up for yourself in these clerical matters must be differentiated from over zealotry and conniving behavior. My cousins have an uncle who since has become estranged from the family through divorce. Since our families were close growing up, I got to know their uncle fairly well and found him to be a bit idiosyncratic. To me, he was an example of someone who leveraged against large companies on clerical matters to extract personal gain. One particular example comes to mind. He and I would often talk about running, as we were both active exercisers. When the subject of running shoes once came up, he bragged how he always gets a new pair of New Balance sneakers without paying for them. Incredulous, I asked how that could be possible. Without shame, he detailed how every six months or so he would mail his running shoes to the company with a note complaining that the shoes were ruined by the rain. He snapped his fingers and smiled. "Like clockwork," he said, they would mail him back a new pair. Why pay for a new pair? He beamed.

Well, one reason to do so is morality. The scheme in which he engaged is built on lies. It may feel good to save money on running shoes but the expense to his integrity, reputation, and possibly freedom (if he is discovered) far outweighs the cost of the shoes. One can only wonder how many other machinations he has hatched. If it does not feel right, then do not do it. Put yourself in the other person's position before acting in a pattern which you may regret at a later point and for a long time.

B. Collections

As the timeless legal wisdom goes, "Possession is ninety percent of the law." It reasons, then, that one who is in possession of monies to which you are entitled may be a formidable opponent. Recouping said funds is therefore fraught with obstacles.

Where do you begin? That depends on the circumstances of the debt. How much is owed? Who owes it? What is the nature of the debt? Let's start with that last question, and you'll see why in a moment. You'll want to stop the debt from accumulating. The best example I can think of is a tenancy. That's also one of the most difficult debts to cut off because, at least in Massachusetts, you need to use the court process to evict a nonpaying tenant. An eviction may take many months to complete, so it makes sense to begin that process immediately upon determining a tenant's delinquency.

Other types of debt are easier to maintain. Loaning money to a deadbeat is a good example. If you are performing services for pay and the other side is failing to comply with the payment schedule, discontinuing work is a preferable option. If, as a consumer, you are paying a bill on a regular basis (e.g. cable, telephone, electricity) and are not receiving the services or the services are not satisfactory, you should consider stopping payment.

So, now you've effectively frozen the debt. At this stage, you should be able to quantify the exact amount owed. Regardless of the size of the arrearage, I would send out a demand letter at this point. What follows is a sample letter a handyman might write to a client who owes him money:

PART II

> Fred Fibble
> 23 County Road
> New City, NY
> 02199
>
> RE: *Contracting Work*
>
> January 1, 2008
>
> Dear Mr. Fibble:
>
> Please know that I have made several efforts to contact you by phone regarding the work I performed in September. As you will note from the invoice I mailed in October, a balance of $750 remains on the account.
> I assume you are satisfied with the quality of the work, as you have not indicated otherwise. Accordingly, please comply with the contract we signed by forwarding payment in the immediate future. Though I don't wish to go that route, please note that should the account remain delinquent by February 1, 2008, I will be forced to turn the matter over to a collection agency.
> It remains my hope to avoid that step.
>
> > Truly Yours,
> > Disappointed Dan

There are several important reasons to write such a letter, some patent and some not so obvious. Clearly, it is possible that the communication will galvanize the person to pay monies owed. Note that my tone is conciliatory. If you use the letter to vent, it will thwart this function. Few people, if any, respond favorably to blame or threats. Be firm but gentle.

If the letter fails to achieve this objective, you will win in other ways by writing it. For one, if the matter ever goes to court, you'll look like Mr. Good Guy by attempting informal resolution. There's also the healthy feeling that attaches to trying to work out differences without the court. The court system, in my view, should be the forum of last resort. Does an honorable black belt in karate rush to the fight? No, it's only when negotiation fails that he seeks the drastic measure of putting his opponent on his backside.

Unfortunately, negotiating payment of a debt through informal means, like the referenced letter, usually fails. Why is that? The obvious answer is that one who owes money will often not take repayment seriously unless the court process is imposed on him or her. He either is disingenuous, knowingly acting to defraud his creditors, hopeless and so self-absorbed that he is oblivious to the havoc his conduct causes, or he may genuinely be unable to pay the debt due to overwhelming personal and/or financial reasons. The last scenario, while worthy of your empathy, is as ineffectual at resolving the problem as are the others.

That means you should prepare for the next step: formal court proceedings. You can also report the debt to a credit bureau, but that action won't recoup your money. Mention of the word 'court,' I've noticed, often throws people in one of two extreme directions. Some folks perceive it in the same manner that they treat topics such as death and income taxes, namely with fear and uncertainty. Others have been involved in courts so many times that they're detached. They are therefore unafraid to pursue the case in the court arena. Where you fit in that spectrum may depend on your experience.

In Massachusetts, where the dollar amount in a dispute is less than $2,000 you can file a small claims complaint. The filing fee is minimal, likely less than $50. The other advantage is that, unlike more involved civil procedures, you get a quick hearing date. At the informal hearing, both sides present their evidence before a clerk magistrate, who typically mails a written decision within a week or two. If you get a judgment and the other side fails to pay, there is an enforcement method and an arrest warrant may issue.

If the amount owed exceeds $2,000, at least in Massachusetts, you'll need to file with a higher court. No need to panic. Remind yourself that collection cases are not complicated legal matters. You are merely alleging breach of contract. In Massachusetts, like most states, the complaint need only contain the fundamental allegations. By using the template I have enclosed (See Appendix) you'll be able to prepare and file most basic collection complaints.

I should submit this disclaimer, so as not to disillusion you: Anyone can be his or her own lawyer. In small or low-level cases, doing so is easier, and your chance of success is higher. No one with a modicum of intelligence, however, would advise pro se representation (e.g. representing yourself) in all cases. Notably, refusing a lawyer in a criminal case or high profile civil case will stuff you in the notorious category of "He who represents himself has a fool for a client." Further, judges often express frustration toward and frown upon self-representation for obvious reasons. For one, non-lawyers are unfamiliar with procedural rules and protocol. For another, a person representing himself may lack the requisite detachment to smoothly pursue the case. We will discuss this subject at length in the tail end of the book.

That said, in the narrow category of collection cases, it might make sense to save the legal fees necessary to hire a lawyer. Of course, the amount in dispute, the nature of the defendant (e.g. small or large corporation), and your personal comfort with the legal process should guide your decision.

C. The Litigation Process in a Nutshell

Of course, litigation is not as simple as filing a complaint. There's much more involved, depending on the complexity of the case. Sections of law libraries are devoted to the intricacies and nuances of litigation. What I'd like to do is merely introduce the most fundamental concepts so that they are recognizable. Here goes: After the complaint is filed, a copy must be served with a summons on the defendant (this form is obtainable from the court). Then the next big step is 'discovery,' in which either side can obtain information from the other through written or live questions. In the simple collections case, the court will likely notify the parties of a 'pretrial conference' within a year of filing—in other cases, it will take longer. At the pretrial conference, a trial date is set. If a jury is necessary, it will be empanelled the day before or the day of the trial. At the trial, both sides present their witnesses and evidence, and the trier of fact (judge or jury) makes a judgment on the disputed issues. The vast majority of cases (something like 98%) never make it to trial. The weak ones are dismissed at earlier stages. Many settle, sometimes immediately after the complaint is filed. The unsuccessful litigant has appellate rights with a higher court.

I will admit it is dangerous to attempt to summarize as broad a topic as litigation. To do otherwise, however, would risk compromising the themes of this book. There are numerous subcategories which I'll merely introduce. One is filing motions. Motions are written requests of the court asking that something be done or prevented. You are 'moving' the court to change a hearing date, extend the time for you to take some action, etc. The other major litigation category worthy of discussion is discovery. In a nutshell, discovery is the means of exchanging information. You can send written questions (interrogatories) to the other side, written requests for documents, statements for the other side to admit or deny (admissions), or ask the other side or nonparty witness live questions under oath (depositions).

PART II

D. Selected Real Estate Matters

I'm sure the word 'selected' in this subtitle caught your attention. It may sound like something a politician would use. True, but I'd be offering poor advice if I encouraged you to represent yourself in all real estate cases.

In what types of real estate cases can you represent yourself? Let's start with the buying and selling of homes. Most people hire a lawyer as a matter of course for these transactions, but it's not always necessary. When you're selling, there's little that can go wrong on your end. Further, if you have a broker, he or she is responsible for preparing the legal forms, getting the final water read, and securing any other requisite documentation.

With sharp negotiating skills and a basic understanding of how these deals work, as the seller, you'll be fine by yourself. In Massachusetts, once the parties agree on a purchase price, the buyer signs the accepted offer. Contingencies for securing a necessary mortgage and for a home inspection are built into this initial agreement.

In the next couple of weeks, the parties will execute the transaction's major document, known as a 'Purchase and Sale Agreement' ("P&S"). The P&S sets forth the firm purchase price, which may be modified from the original, agreed-upon figure depending on what the inspection uncovers. Incidentally, paying a few hundred dollars for a home inspection is essential. The inspector may find conditions such as mold or electrical wiring problems, which you would never notice yourself.

Once you iron down a final purchase price, modified or not from the initial negotiations, you are ready to sign the P&S. Contemporaneous with the execution will be your down payment of up to 20% of the purchase price. The only remaining step before the closing is your securing a mortgage (if you are the buyer). It's important that the buyer be certain about the deal before signing the P&S. Why? Because his down payment will be difficult to recover. Unless the house burns down or the seller has a true moment of magnanimity (by agreeing to void the deal and return the funds), the buyer will forfeit the down payment.

The final step, the closing, consummates the deal. The seller, through his lawyer, his broker or himself if he attends without representation, signs over the title to the house in exchange for what remains of the purchase price. The closing takes place either at the office of the mortgage attorney or the Registry of Deeds where the new deed will be filed.

The buyer will be more active in the closing, as he will be signing upwards of fifty documents presented by his mortgage company's lawyer. Some forms are essential (such as the promissory note), while others are silly (like a form which says the mortgage company can make any changes to the documents caused by a mistake on their part). All the forms the bank lawyer submits to the buyer for his signature are similar in one respect: They serve to protect the bank's interest beyond doubt in the event the buyer defaults. I joke with my buyer clients that each of the documents they sign will be an exhibit in any necessary court proceedings.

What are potential trouble-spots with home sales? As suggested, the buyer has more to lose. The seller leaves the closing with a nice cashier's check, money in hand. Nothing can go wrong with what he receives. The buyer is not so fortunate. He gets a home, which based on a home inspection and title search, reveals no problems. Yet, such an investigation is not absolute.

In the context of condominiums, a buyer needs to review the condo documents and finances with care. Is there an imminent, major building project? If so, the new owner may bear a percentage of the cost. Some examples of expensive building projects are: replacing an air conditioner tower, upgrading an elevator, and re-pointing the outside of the building. Make sure the condominium reserves are healthy and review the expenditures of the prior few years to determine whether the association has been frugal. Another point of inquiry is whether the condo fees have recently been raised or are expected to be increased anytime soon. To that end, obtaining the phone numbers of the condo trustees and calling as many as you can would be wise.

Your common sense is a helpful tool in deciding whether to purchase a house or condo. You certainly don't need a lawyer for that. In fact, anyone who has dealt with lawyers knows what I'm talking about. Lawyers and common sense are often unrelated. That said, interview neighbors. Walk around the neighborhood if you're not familiar with it. Try a local restaurant or two and time the walk to public transportation if that's an issue. If you feel such research is unnecessary, consider how much money you are investing in this purchase, and then reconsider. There's no such thing as a waste of time in this context.

If you're purchasing a multi-family home in which one or more tenants reside, you have an added concern. That's because, as the new landlord, you inherit any problems the prior owner had with the tenants. Many buyers are either lazy or naïve in limiting their research to questioning the seller. "What are the tenants like?" they'll ask. "Oh good," the seller will respond. "Never had any problems."

A wise buyer will add a paragraph or two to the P&S, which requires the seller to memorialize this representation. The better practice, I believe, is to get a copy of the lease in advance and to contact the city or town inspectional department to see if the tenant has lodged complaints. You can also contact the clerk's office of your local court to ascertain whether the seller has ever filed an eviction case.

The other sound approach is to insist on obtaining the tenant's phone number to set up a face-to-face meeting before signing the P&S and making the large down payment that accompanies it. Lyndon B. Johnson, as you may know, was our 36th President. He was also an expert at reading people. He subscribed to a theory developed by his father, also a politician. In essence, it went like this: If you can't walk into a room and tell within minutes who is for you and who is against you, you don't belong in politics. By analogy, a landlord who cannot distinguish a good prospective tenant from a bad one within minutes will struggle as a landlord. Inheriting a bad tenant could have disastrous consequences; the eviction process is often hard and expensive. We'll discuss that route in a few minutes.

A final issue to consider is financing. I'm no mortgage broker, but there are a few nuggets of wisdom which I have gathered from my personal and professional experiences. First of all, shop for the best rate, but make sure you know what the closing costs will be. Whether to choose a standard fixed mortgage or an adjustable one should be a function of your circumstances and goals. Remember that your rate may rise if you opt for an adjustable rate mortgage ("ARM").

Disputes with Contractors

Again, I speak from a Massachusetts vantage point. If you live in Nevada, Oklahoma, Washington, Illinois, or any other state, you'll need to check their rules and laws. Here, homeowners need not avail themselves of the time-consuming, expensive, and unpredictable legal system.

Instead, if they believe a home improvement contractor has either poorly-performed work or failed to complete a project, they may file papers with an administrative entity in the Attorney General's office. What's the advantage? For one, it encourages resolution by removing the impediment of protracted litigation. How many people have you heard expressing disillusionment and capitulation in the face of paying an expensive attorney retainer and waiting a few years to get a trial date? So, you save money and time. The other advantage is ensuring the contractor's presence at the hearing. The state agency has the authority to take action on the contractor's license.

PART II

<u>Defective Car Purchases</u>

We have administrative avenues which are also available to automobile consumers who have purchased 'lemons'. They get a quick (and binding) decision from an arbitrator which may require an auto dealer to refund the entire cost of the vehicle. The process parallels that of the contractor dispute. Forms and information are available on state consumer web sites. Again, I have not researched how all other states operate, but my instinct tells me they similarly value the interests and rights of consumers. You can also easily access your state's Lemon Laws which may provide for punitive damages against the dealer.

<u>Landlord/Tenant Issues</u>

As we've seen, you don't need a lawyer for everything. In fact, with many transactions and in numerous proceedings, you can represent yourself as effectively as a high-paid lawyer could. Just keep calm and think in common sense, simple terms.

That's been the essence of my message.

Landlord/tenant disputes run the gamut: from tenant complaints about conditions in the apartment to alleged security deposit violations to evictions. With respect to the majority of these matters, my view is that you don't need to be a lawyer to succeed.

This book is far from an authoritative 'how to' book when it comes to any of the legal areas we address. That concept may resonate in this section. In Massachusetts, as in perhaps other states as well, housing laws are favorable to tenants. This is fact, not a matter of opinion, evidenced by the many expert legal commentators who have acknowledged as much. Therefore, without a good knowledge of specifics, general principles may prove to be false friends. Be sure to review a handbook on housing law if you intend to represent yourself in matters concerning your tenants.

In the Appendix, I've included a residential lease which covers the essential components you'll need. Remember that the careful and wise selection of tenants is no substitute for a well-drafted lease.

Building Code Matters

Different towns may have varying ways of handling these matters, but the gist is the same: The landowner is compelled to fix conditions in the unit of which the tenant has complained. Sometimes the alleged violations are of a serious nature (e.g. furnace not functioning in the winter or rodent infestation) while in others the complaints are easily remediable.

Generally, the code enforcement agents (e.g. the city or town inspectors) are obligated to work with landlords who have allegedly violated the code. This fact, coupled with the relative simplicity of these proceedings, means landlords are usually fine representing themselves. It reasons that the overwhelming majority of building code proceedings are resolved through the landlord's ultimate compliance.

If you are a landlord of a building in which significant and numerous allegations of disrepair are alleged and you are unable to secure contractors to make timely repairs, you may need to consult an attorney.

E. Some Family Law & Probate Cases

Child Support

In my experience, delinquent dads escape their child support responsibility because of the mother's fear and perhaps misapprehension of the process. Mothers usually call a handful of lawyers to help them pursue financial support from these unconscionable dads. The problem is that since these victimized mothers don't have money to pay legal fees, they're left to their own devices. So, they give up, feeling defeated by an unfair system.

Whenever I get a call on one of these cases, I encourage the person to pursue a child support order on her own. "I can't do it," she'll say. "Yes you can," I respond. Massachusetts is not unique in taking a strong stand against deadbeat dads. Reciprocity runs strong among states, so if the deadbeat tries to skip off to Oklahoma, it may be tougher to collect on him. You will, however, find it much easier than you would with other types of collection cases.

So, how do you get a support order? The key is to know the residential address of your child's deadbeat father. Sadly, in many of these cases, the deadbeat leaves town (sometimes even the country). Obviously in that example he leaves no trail as to his whereabouts, so unless you can discover it on your own there is no means of serving him and therefore no means of collecting.

If you have an address, then you would file a complaint in the probate/family court where you live. Typically, there is no filing fee for such cases, saving you upwards of two hundred dollars. I suggest you go to the court and speak with a friendly-looking clerk. He or she can walk you through the protocol of that court/state/jurisdiction. Follow his or her instructions to schedule a hearing before the judge. At the hearing, the judge should sign an order requiring the defendant to pay a certain monthly or weekly amount, based on his income, your income and the needs of the child. It is generally preferable to get an order of support from the court versus agreeing (informally) to the dad's paying a certain monthly or weekly sum. The reasons are two-fold: For one, the informal offer will likely be less than he should be required to pay, but secondly (and more importantly) courts provide a means of enforcement.

If the deadbeat does not respond to the order by paying, you will need to go back to court for a contempt order. When successful, the court will issue a warrant for the deadbeat and haul him into court. If they can ascertain his whereabouts, they will detain him until he pays at least some of the child support arrearage. In my experience, most of the deadbeats in shackles find a way to get the money. It's also interesting how apologetic they are at that point.

Probating a Will or Seeking Appointment as an Administrator

If you've been named as the executor in someone's will and that person dies, you are responsible for filing the will in the probate court where the person died and for notifying all interested parties (e.g. those who are named beneficiaries under the terms of the will and all heirs or potential heirs).

The prior paragraph sounds more complicated than it is. In most instances, there aren't many interested parties and the estate has a relatively low value. Therefore, don't rush to pay a lawyer when you can handle the probating on your own. Some lawyers' fees are a percentage of the estate's value. If the estate were worth $200,000, would you want to pay a lawyer 5% ($10,000) to do what you are capable of doing?

Instead of hiring a lawyer, contact a friendly clerk at your local probate court. Going there for an in-person discussion may prove to be a valuable investment. In Boston, a so-called 'lawyer of the day' sits at a desk in the clerk's office and provides free legal advice. He or she can provide you with forms you will need to probate the case and instructions on how to get the necessary death certificate.

Petitioning for administration requires an extra step, namely securing appointments as administrator of the decedent's estate. You'll need to file a petition for administration where the decedent did not have a will. Usually a family member of the decedent files for appointment as administrator, and the request is allowed without opposition by most judges. The notable exception occurs in family squabbles, often where the siblings are at odds.

Again, the forms are readily available at your local probate court, as is the assistance of a clerk. Since many clerks work in every court, like all people, they often have personalities which run the gamut. Your quest, when you go there, will be to find one who does not appear to be weighted down by a bad mood, a gruff mannerism, or a general sense of uncooperativeness. Instead, look for one who smiles and laughs with regularity. He or she may be pleased to help you out and may even provide some insight as to the functioning of that particular court.

Modifications and No-Fault Divorces

A complaint for modification in Massachusetts works as follows: A party to a divorce, custody, or support case has signed an agreement or received a judgment from the court. At some later point, maybe six months, a year, two years or however long, the moving party may feel that his or her life circumstances have changed (or the other side's have changed) such that the terms of the agreement should be changed. It reasons that the party seeking the modification bears the burden of proving the dramatic change in circumstances.

What are some reasons why a party would seek modification of an existing order or judgment? Let's examine custody. At the time of the trial in a divorce case, say the minor children are living with their mother and doing well. The trial judge will likely award physical custody to the mother, meaning the children will continue to reside with her. Now, if the mother has some sort of mental breakdown in the near future, requiring hospitalization for instance, her custody award is in jeopardy. If the father is capable of caring for them, he may file the complaint to modify the existing order.

The father can get the forms from his local probate court and follow any written instructions that may appear on the package. Essentially, he needs to complete an affidavit, which sets forth the facts he claims form the basis for his modification request. He'll also need to provide basic information on the complaint. Then, he can mark the case up for a hearing to get a temporary order and make the argument before the judge when that date arrives. Hiring a qualified lawyer will no doubt help your chances of prevailing, especially if the other side has one. But at what cost? My guess is that a family law attorney would request a retainer of at least $5,000 to get started. My suggestion is to begin without an attorney. There is some risk that you could damage your case by representing yourself at the beginning, but this typically only occurs when you provide a sworn statement in an affidavit or deposition. Therefore, avoid doing so without a lawyer's review. If the matter becomes too complicated or contentious, you can always hire a lawyer at a later point.

Let me be clear about representing yourself in a divorce action: There are only specific circumstances under which I so advise. If there are any disputes between the parties on any issues (e.g. custody, division of assets, etc.), my recommendation is that you consult with an attorney. If you cannot afford one, there are free legal service agencies which may assist. Particularly where the parties are mired in protracted disputes, I believe the services of a seasoned divorce attorney are indispensable. Navigating through divorce laws, procedure, and strategy is difficult enough for one qualified to do so; to place that burden on a non-lawyer who is emotionally tangled in the dispute is risky.

Now might be an appropriate time to further clarify an important point. Being self-reliant, standing up for yourself when the self-serving forces of corporations and bureaucracy obstruct, and saving the thousands of dollars in legal fees you'll often spend when hiring an attorney are general rules. These are guidelines. You may be able to remove a splinter from your foot by using tweezers and some rubbing alcohol, but would you attempt to do the same with a dangerous-looking mole? Or administer a vaccine? Of course not. You'd see your doctor. The same applies to legal issues; many things you can do on your own, while some require a lawyer's involvement. There are limits.

So let's talk about the 'line' in distinguishing when you can and cannot represent yourself. If your ex and you seem to be in agreement on most issues and he or she has secured an attorney to discuss what's in dispute, be concerned. It is irrelevant how nice and courteous the attorney appears to be. Remember, whenever an attorney contacts you to negotiate under disputed circumstances you must be cautious. A good lawyer can draft an agreement which appears innocuous on its face but whose meaning can be changed by inserting or removing a word or two. Unscrupulous lawyers will take advantage of their heightened knowledge and training with respect to legal documents, so you'll have to be aware.

Where there are no disagreements, you can obtain and prepare the necessary uncontested divorce forms at your local probate court. You and the other party must execute a series of documents, which may vary depending on your state's requirements. In Massachusetts, where children are involved, both parties are required to attend parenting classes. Once the forms are filed and the clerk's fee paid, the court schedules a hearing date in which the judge reviews the documents to ensure the divorce terms are reasonable. Then, in a short period of time, the divorce becomes final.

F. Claims Involving Insurance Companies

Everyone is familiar with the notorious television ads of personal injury lawyers, as well as the billboards and <u>Yellow Pages</u>. They portray the injured party as a victim, the insurance companies as monsters, and themselves as saviors. These extreme stereotypes persuade many people into believing they are helpless in those cases without the assistance of an astute tort lawyer.

If the injuries are serious, you would be smart to consult a lawyer. Remember though, that the standard lawyer fee is one-third of the settlement. Where the injuries are of a soft tissue nature (e.g. neck and back) and there is no issue of liability (e.g. the other vehicle or entity is clearly at fault), you may be best served by processing the claim yourself.

Call up a lawyer you know or conduct some independent research to find out what your case may be worth. Massachusetts is different from other states in that we have no fault insurance in car accident cases. It works like this: When you're injured in a car accident, your insurance company will (with limited exceptions) pay your medical expenses and seventy-five percent of lost wages up to $8,000.

These cases are relatively easy to process. You fill out the required paperwork with your insurance company and seek treatment for your injuries. When you're done with treatment, you forward all bills and records to the at-fault insurance carrier with a demand. This discussion brings us to the fundamental question in injury cases: How much is it worth? In responding, I can only speak in ranges, since there are so many random variables for which you cannot account (e.g. the reputation of the insurance company, the quality of the medical records, the credibility of the witnesses, and the like).

That said, allow me to provide some guidelines. For soft tissue injuries you can expect a settlement offer of between three and seven thousand dollars. Of course, if there are liability issues or questionable treatment, those figures may vary. If you hire a lawyer to take one-third of your settlement, you can do the math.

If your injuries are more severe, unusual, or if the insurance company fights you, necessitating litigation, you should consult an attorney. In those situations, by opting to do it yourself you jeopardize the probability of achieving a fair settlement or judgment. There's no way I (in the limited context of this modest book) or even an author of a five hundred-page text on the subject could train you for such an endeavor. Remember that not all lawyers are competent, as is true of any professional. Nonetheless, even the worst lawyer will have completed three years of law school and had some practical experience, which is more expertise than you can claim unless you are a professional litigant. What's more is the stark financial reality concerning insurance companies. When it comes to money, insurance companies have a lot of it, much more than you do. Further, they're more inclined to throw it at their lawyers than they are to settle with you. Can you see where I'm going with this? While in my experience insurance lawyers are often hacks, they have the resources to make your life difficult—especially if you're representing yourself.

Malpractice claims against doctors, hospitals, and other medical providers also fall in the "don't touch by yourself" category. In Massachusetts, and I would presume most states, these matters are defended by more sophisticated insurance lawyers than you would find in other cases. They rarely settle unless the case is quite strong and you've mired them in litigation for a long time. The second reason to hire counsel to represent you in medical malpractice cases concerns experts: You will need to retain a doctor or other qualified health practitioner to cite the alleged incidents of malpractice. These experts are reluctant, in my experience, to get involved in pro-se cases.

Property Damage Claims

Property damage claims are viable for self-representation. Remember, insurance companies are regulated by most states to be reasonable in settling claims. If they fail to do so, there may be financial and criminal consequences. With claims under homeowner's policies, I've noticed insurers tend to rely on vague language in being stingy. For example, if a flood causes extensive damage to your basement, your carrier may reject your request for reimbursement of a contractor's bill it labels as "unreasonable". If the gross bill is only slightly more than they're willing to pay, you may be able to negotiate a resolution.

Getting reimbursed for damage to your vehicle is another issue. The dispute often concerns liability and coverage. Here's how it plays out: When another vehicle causes damage to yours, you must secure the other operator's insurance information. If you have a deductible for damage to your vehicle, you can coordinate reimbursement through your insurance carrier. In this instance, your insurance company will front the money for repair work and then seek reimbursement from the at-fault carrier. People often become concerned that involving their insurance companies will adversely affect their premiums. This is untrue. As long as you have not been cited or determined to be at fault in an accident, your rates should not be affected.

If you don't have a deductible for damage caused to your vehicle, your insurance company will not get involved. You will need to coordinate directly with the at-fault carrier, a more challenging task. Why is that? The most compelling reason is that your insurance company, to whom you make payments, is not involved in the negotiations. So, if they are absent from the discussions you may lose this power of persuasion. Another advantage to having your insurance agent negotiate instead of you is the fact that they work in the industry and are more versed with the process than you are. That doesn't mean you shouldn't monitor their work on the matter.

Does this mean that without your insurance agent's involvement all is lost? Of course not. If there is no dispute as to liability, chances are good you will succeed in securing the at-fault carrier's payment of your auto damages. The key is to contact them right after the collision so that their appraiser can come assess the damage before you begin repair work. Too many times, people will take pictures of the damage, believing that to be 'proof,' and then have the work done prior to contacting the insurance agent. They're devastated when told they won't get reimbursement, but they have no recourse. Don't make that mistake.

If the at-fault carrier disputes liability or low balls you (a favorite phrase of personal injury lawyers), be prepared to fight. Get informal statements from witnesses or an invoice from your auto body shop and attach them to a demand letter you will send to the insurance adjuster. As discussed in passing above, insurance companies doing business in Massachusetts are bound by tough consumer protection laws. In short, insurance companies must be 'reasonable' in settling claims. Further, they must promptly investigate and evaluate matters which you bring to their attention. If they fail to do so and you send them a well-written demand letter, a court may grant you triple damages, attorneys' fees, and costs. More importantly, since litigation is onerous, the demand letter serves as a valuable negotiating tool. The other important requirement in Massachusetts is that the insurance company must respond within 30 days. Many of the larger insurers have in-house attorneys, so there's no additional expense for them to draft a demand letter response. With others, however, hiring private defense counsel is necessary. Hopefully, you get my point here. Rather than pay an attorney's fee to respond to your letter, the financial practicalities may persuade them to settle your claim. I've included a sample consumer demand letter in the Appendix.

Let me end this section with a common theme when it comes to representing yourself versus hiring an attorney. Here it is: As you've noticed, I generally encourage you to represent yourself on less complicated matters, where the money in dispute is somewhat insignificant. It follows that were a lawyer to take on your somewhat insignificant monetary dispute, he or she would not afford it priority statues.

So why should you hire a lawyer on these matters?

G. Everyday Disputes

In this category, the issue is no longer whether you need an attorney to represent your interests. Rather, the challenge is effectively advocating to secure your objectives. I suppose my use of 'everyday' in the title to this chapter is overworked. What we're really talking about here are matters of moderate to minimal significance. We're not talking about courts (judges, juries, etc.). Nor are we dealing with particularly large sums of money.

Nonetheless, there are opportunities to correct mistakes and save money and aggravation. What kinds of disputes are we talking about? Let's take a look.

Store Bills

Be honest with yourself. When you make a store purchase do you check the math on the receipt? So what, you say. What's a dollar or two on occasion; it's not worth the aggravation. There are irritable people waiting behind you.

So the argument goes.

Consider the amount of time most people spend accumulating coupons, shopping for sales, and the like. If you'd feel rushed taking a few extra moments reviewing a bill, imagine how stressed the cashier must be. His supervisor may be breathing on him, pressuring him to move faster through your items. You, in contrast, merely have the irascible people behind you with whom to contend. None of them has the power to do anything except stare at you in a peculiar way or perhaps make an insulting comment like, "C'mon, pick up the pace."

My point with the cashier being stressed is that in such a fast-paced environment, he or she is likely to err. It happens with more frequency then you might think. The other fact to consider is that, excuse me if this sounds patronizing or elitist, but cashier positions are (to be gentle) transitory jobs. The educational and skill thresholds, not to mention salary, are low. This means that, as a general rule, cashiers may lack the attention to detail you would find in a more coveted position.

Returns

My philosophy lies somewhere between yahoo and Puritan when it comes to complaining about a meal or a malfunctioning television. Yahoos abuse the temporary power they wield as 'customers' by over-playing this positioning. We've all known and seen such disrepute. They will eat half of their meal at a fancy restaurant and then complain that it is not cooked well, manipulating the waitress into bringing a second serving. These same types will engage in other sleazy activities to maximize their savings (and enjoyment).

The group I have labeled "Puritans" exercises an abundance

of restraint when it comes to self-advocacy. They deem it undignified to complain, even in instances where their humble objectives are easily-justified. Most of the time, these folks were taught or learned that etiquette and suppression of feelings were co-dependent concepts. These repressed folks invariably find alternative receptacles for their snowballing anger. They may explode at a child, spouse, or co-worker. It follows that, at least in my view, the Puritanical approach with its rather useless concept of nobility fails on many levels.

We're brought to the middle ground approach, which I encourage. I must admit that I gravitate toward the restraint end, but I will complain on occasion—particularly when the product I've purchased is expensive. With meals, unless it's raw or half-eaten, I'll keep my figurative and literal mouth shut.

The key point in this discussion pertains to the most effective mechanism of complaining. How you voice your concern is more important than when you do it. I notice that both the yahoo and the Puritan react in an uncomfortable fashion, yielding poor results. With the yahoo, we're often talking about an unhappy loser, someone who fails at most everything he tries and who needs attention. If his top sirloin is slightly overcooked, he'll call the waiter over and jabber about the chef's poor cooking performance or how disgusted he is as a regular restaurant customer when in reality, he frequents fast food joints with more regularity. He abuses the deference most restaurants afford their patrons. In short, the yahoo is often unstable to begin with, meaning something minor like an overcooked steak can set him off. His reaction embarrasses the waiter, chef, and his guests (unless they're of his cut). He'll likely get another dinner, though the short-term success will encourage future theatrics. Over time, he'll grow a poor reputation.

When the Puritan spends a winter night in a hotel room and the heat malfunctions or the radiator is so loud that he can't sleep, he'll repress his feelings of indignation. The better approach, I believe, is to call the front desk and in a pleasant voice (which may be hard to muster under the circumstances) detail the concern and express some empathy toward them (e.g. the fact that there's only one person handling all of the hotel's business at that hour). If you have the Puritan's instincts, like me, you'll need to remind yourself that you're paying for a hotel room. You are entitled to a functioning heating system and relative quiet while you sleep. You are not a 'complainer', so long as you advocate in a professional and fair manner.

It's important to separate your emotions from the task at hand. I find myself repeating the concept with some regularity. Using the convenient example of the hotel room, say you encounter a less-than-nice staff person who resists your requests for assistance. Further, assume the individual suggests you are over-reacting or that there is nothing he or she can do to ameliorate the situation. Raising your voice, mimicking the manipulative or insensitive behavior, or even threatening, must be eliminated as responsive options. By attaching your emotions to the equation you will likely empower the unreasonable/belligerent/malignant individual with whom you are dealing. In addition, your own sense of worth may be dictated by this individual whom you hold in low esteem.

H. Dealing With the Police

With my law degree and training, I would be considered more sophisticated than most when it comes to understanding my Constitutional rights. But I must admit that the sight of an armed police officer makes me a bit reluctant to tout such knowledge. Further, I have maintained a certain idealism since childhood which encourages me to assume all police officers are professional, caring, and competent. Sadly, like with every profession, an unqualified, mentally unstable, or self-serving percentage infiltrates. When individuals carry firearms and have the power to physically detain us, it is scary to think of their incompetence or personality defects. We must understand our fundamental rights, so that if confronted by an officer who abuses his power (for whom we pay tax dollars), we can preserve our liberty. What follows is an overview of some basic Constitutional rights and criminal law concepts.

Fourth Amendment ("Search and Seizure")

Most people would comply with a police officer's request for entrance if he knocked at their door. The Fourth Amendment, though, prohibits access to your home, automobile or any possessions without probable cause. The general rule is that they need to obtain a search warrant from a court magistrate. Notable exceptions include emergencies and cases where you are arrested for another reason and the officer notices evidence of criminality.

Why should you deny access if you have nothing to hide? Won't that look suspicious? Good questions. My best answer is a simple one: You don't need to. It's aggravating and stressful, not to mention a waste of your time, to meet with the police. Further, even though you may not be on their radar in terms of culpability, they can still impose nightmares on your life. As much as we'd like to think otherwise, law enforcement agents often have an agenda, namely to find a guilty person. If they can't find someone, you may be their choice. Don't take any chances by assuming they're only interested in fairness and truth.

Alternatively, you could become a witness in future proceedings, requiring you to expend money on attorneys' fees and/or lose days or weeks from work to testify. It's also important to note that your silence cannot be construed as an admission of culpability. Bear in mind that prosecution and law enforcement are careers characterized by punishment and power. They can bring out the extremes of good and bad in people. If you are forthcoming in answering too many questions, an overzealous law enforcement agent (and they abound) may prey on your candor, twist the facts, and/or pressure you to give names of others who may not want to speak.

Remember the Fourth Amendment is our protection as individuals against the creation of a police state. You don't need to justify the invocation of this right beyond reminding whoever questions you that it exists in our Constitution. If it was good enough for the Framers, shouldn't that suffice? The burden for searching is on the officer who wants to look. Thankfully, we do not live in a police state where law enforcement officials are given blanket power to search as they wish.

I'm sure you've read about high-profile criminal cases in which a defendant is exonerated because the police conducted an illegal search or entered a home without a warrant. The items obtained, like drugs or firearms, are suppressed from introduction as evidence at trial. Many people are indignant to learn a likely conviction is lost or overturned on appeal on one of these bases. I agree but would say that without this check on police power, more bad will come than good. If the police knew they were immune, their investigations could all be witch-hunts, and they could disrupt lives without consequence for mistakes. We need to preserve basic privacy and other individual rights.

Miranda Rights

Here we're talking about your rights if arrested. Notably, as everyone sees on television, you are entitled to refuse to speak with the police and to have court-appointed counsel if you cannot afford a lawyer. Don't kid yourself into thinking the police will hold your hand and answer questions you may have regarding what <u>Miranda</u> means. Forget it. They will often blurt out the famous words of warning and then cajole a detained individual into making gratuitous remarks, hoping to yield a confession or statements to implicate others. Often, they will (and the law permits) resort to under-handed means. To some degree, I believe that they should be afforded some leeway so that hardened criminals are brought to justice. I am far from an ideologue willing to allow criminals to undercut our wonderful and fair system of justice. It pains me, for instance, when a pedophile is exonerated because of a police error.

The answer, I believe, is for policemen and women to receive the proper training so that they can respect our individual rights and freedoms while prosecuting criminals. But what if the criminal conduct is rather obvious (e.g. five bags of cocaine discovered in a crack house) in cases where the police screw up? Shouldn't there be exceptions? Well, there are exceptions, which our courts have carved out. Consider the danger of giving in too frequently to police mistakes. I cannot imagine I stand alone in feeling anxious at the prospect of the police entering my home for any arbitrary reason or even on mere suspicion. Similarly, the idea of a whimsical arrest is odious.

Routine Car Stops & Related Matters

Not that long ago, I was standing outside my former home in downtown Boston, returning from a Sunday morning run. It's a one-way street, and I was facing the intersection from which cars are prohibited from entering. Suddenly, a black SUV turned illegally onto the street at a high speed. Since young children (including my own) and elderly adults often walk on the street, I was angered at the traffic violation and threw my hands in the air before gesticulating (peacefully) at the vehicle. The window rolled down and a uniformed police officer barked out, "You gotta problem?" I was stunned and admittedly a bit phased by his status and loud words. So, I froze in silence. He added, "That's what I thought," laughed, and then sped off. At no point was his emergency siren sounding, leading me to the conclusion that he was abusing his power as a police officer in breaking the law. If I had the moment back, I think I would have questioned his conduct in a non-emergency situation and perhaps apprised him of my status as a lawyer. Also, I might have committed his license plate to memory and reported it to the local precinct.

Why do I share this story? Well, it's not to generalize about police officers. I could tell you more instances of professionalism and consideration. My view, though, is that police must be held to a much higher standard, primarily because they carry weapons. These weapons, if improperly or frivolously used, can end innocent lives. In other words, their mistakes can cause fatalities.

My message is to remain vigilant of police abuse and overreaching so that you may gently confront it when necessary. It follows that you should refrain from acts of stupidity. These seem most prominent in the context of ordinary traffic stops. Bedside manners, I understand, are not taught at the police academy. So don't expect a cop to shake your hand or make small talk upon approaching your vehicle.

If he accuses you of drinking, demands you get out of the vehicle or acts unprofessionally, you should turn the questions on him. Calmly ask him for the basis of his request. Always keep in mind that you have no legal obligation to answer questions, permit a search unless you see a warrant, or submit to field sobriety tests. If he refuses to produce a warrant, then ask for his badge number and explain that you can't comply. Breathalyzer tests are a tricky thing. If you know that you will likely be over the .08 blood alcohol limit, then it seems obvious that you should refuse the test. However, in some states, refusing to take the test results in an automatic suspension of your license for a longer period of time than if you take the test and fail. Doesn't seem fair does it? Those rules vary from state to state, so it would be beneficial to know the laws in your state because if you ever find yourself in that position, there won't be a lot of time to weigh your options. Even though the process is rather quick, ask to call a lawyer before you decide what to do, as they can advise you based on the laws of your state.

These may seem to be bold moves, but I conveniently apprise them that as a practicing lawyer I am aware of my rights. It's easier to be brave in that regard. It also helps to have someone in the car to witness the shenanigans. At the same time, do not antagonize. Be courteous and even-tempered when questioning the cop's decision to pull you over. Even if your verbal remonstrations fail, you will have two more opportunities, as discussed earlier; the first is with the clerk magistrate and the second is before the judge.

I. A Word on Avoiding Legal Engagements

What a strange and inconsistent section, you may think. I'll admit 'avoiding' and 'engaging' in legal matters are conflicting concepts, though I believe it necessary to address the former. When it comes to Due Process and the pursuit of justice (as loaded as that term has become), please know that I endeavor to embrace them in whole and without reservation. Regarding the mechanism of enforcement, I'm more conservative.

I'll break it down further with examples. An effective (and honorable) black belt in karate will only attack as a last resort to solving the problem. Likewise with a skilled debater and his or her words, and a five-star general and his military. These experts in their respective fields exercise restraint, leaving the red meat approach to the numerous yahoos who mistakenly believe muscle-flexing works in the long term. Why is that? These wise experts realize that over-use of their skills, while effective as a short-term solution, wastes energy and creates resentment. In the long-term, therefore, caution is preferable.

How do you avoid legal entanglements, controversies, involvements, and the like? First, don't pursue justice for the sake of it—even if you may be right. You must be zealous and persistent in advocating for yourself, but only when necessary. Professional litigants are notorious and irritate judges and court staff in the same way he or she who repeatedly badgers the local police with 'concerns' which can be independently resolved becomes vilified by that precinct. You think a restaurant will be excited to see you if you've returned poorly-cooked food more than once?

In addition to the exercise of restraint, be nice and pleasant—even to those who do not deserve such courtesy. Doing so will remove you from their radar and decrease the likelihood anyone will instigate with you. Consider the time-tested maxim: He who looks for trouble typically finds it.

Next, before commencing any type of action or registering a claim or complaint, weigh the value of doing so. You may achieve a short-term gain but lose in the more important longer run. Using a personal example, we recently purchased a home outside of Boston. Since it was new construction, under Massachusetts law we obtained a one-year warranty as to any defects in the house. The developer was obligated to promptly fix any problems. After a month or two, we noticed a few items and contacted him. He did not return our messages and I considered writing a firm letter to him. I held off, believing that doing so might affect our relatively good rapport to that point so I was willing to afford him a few more chances. I left three subsequent messages which were conciliatory and expressed understanding for what could have been causing the delay, namely his unavailability. He returned the third call, apologized, and arranged an appointment to fix the items. My patience and belief that seeking 'justice' at that point would have alienated him in the future if we needed him to promptly fix a problem proved correct.

Some might think that you negotiate with strength and that filing a lawsuit or sending a harsh demand letter connotes seriousness. I agree and disagree. I agree that strength is an important show to your opponent. Defining the term may be a point of contention between this line of thinking and mine. It might be a product of my experience as a trial lawyer; knowing how time-consuming and expensive the court process can be has forced me to be more practical. At the same time, I'm more aware of the human element and have learned (through prior errors in judgment) that kindness does more than kill people— it can actually make them feel good and eager to comply with your requests.

There is a line, though, which separates appeasement and

PART II

enablement of bad behavior or bad people and what I'm talking about in the above paragraph. As is the case with most such demarcations, this one is a matter of subjectivity. If and when you need to ramp up your pursuit of justice through formal means is a matter for you to decide.

I'm merely encouraging you to exhaust the easier remedies before going that route.

To paraphrase Benjamin Franklin: "Doing so will make you healthier, wealthier and wiser."

PART III

WHEN YOU NEED A LAWYER

When you've exhausted your ability to represent yourself without compromising your position, it's time to hire an attorney. The question then becomes: How do you know when the time is right? The answer can be found by recognizing when representing yourself would disservice your interests and by being honest in assessing your abilities and experience in self-advocacy. In other words, and I apologize to the concrete thinkers out there, you'll need to meditate a bit in reaching an accurate and satisfying answer.

The next quest is finding an appropriate lawyer. You will need to apply those same self-advocacy skills to this endeavor. Remember that you are paying the lawyer for his/her services. As such you are entitled to the benefit of your bargain, namely a knowledgeable, compassionate and diligent attorney who keeps you apprised of all developments. Interview several candidates, both on the phone and in person if need be. Ask many questions to gauge whether he or she is a good fit for your legal needs. If the lawyer appears too controlling or reluctant to answer your questions, move on to the next one.

There are approximately one million lawyers in the United States, so it shouldn't be too difficult to find prospects. Ask friends, do web searches, call referral services, anything to find an appropriate attorney. This section will address the areas where I believe you need a lawyer and then discuss in somewhat general terms what that specialized lawyer should be doing to protect your interests.

A. Significant Injury Cases

In the last section, we discussed how you could save the one-third or even forty percent attorney's fees in so-called soft tissue cases by representing yourself. Once you've learned the process, understand the valuation system, and appreciate that insurance companies are motivated to settle cases, you can equal, or at least approximate, the work of most personal injury attorneys.

Such is not the case where you are talking about higher impact/serious injury cases. More money is involved and so much more is at stake, both for the insurance companies and the injured parties. Since most of those cases are not resolved, at least not for a fair settlement amount, without filing suit, you will need to hire competent counsel. The template complaints you'll see in the Appendix are light years more simple than complaints in these cases. You can imagine how many depositions, motions, documents, and experts are involved. In short, without the proper training and expertise to litigate significant injury cases, you will likely lose a lot of money. Because of their significant financial exposure, you can expect that competent insurance defense counsel will spend countless hours on litigation techniques which would overwhelm a novice and defeat a non-lawyer.

What is a 'significant' injury? In my view, that covers all injuries which require more than physical therapy or chiropractic attention. This category includes broken bones, nerve damage, scarring, or death. Consider the fact that the insurance company lawyers know that as a non-lawyer you are unfamiliar with the painstaking particularities and time-sensitive deadlines (some of which are fatal in cases of noncompliance) inherent to

PART III

litigation. So, if you try to file a lawsuit for significant injuries you would need to read the <u>Cliffs Notes</u> on practicing law. That, as we know, is an impossible proposition, so pardon my sarcasm.

Once you've met the threshold of significant injury, research local personal injury lawyers through advertisements, word-of-mouth, or past experience. I'd narrow your list to four or five lawyers, exercising caution in avoiding the slick catch-phrases and exaggerations for which, sadly yet realistically, most PI lawyers are known. Here are some sound bites, which should disqualify prospects:

1. Any use of the words "compassionate" and "caring;"
2. Emphasis on free consultation or free representation unless successful; (Remember that practically all personal injury work is contingent or free unless successful. There's no need to over-emphasize that point);
3. Ads which promote toughness or which flaunt a hired hit-man (e.g. a professional actor) to stand in the place of any lawyer in the law firm. One would wonder why the lawyer is not 'tough' enough to pose for the pictures.

Next, you will need to interview your final four or five candidates. Don't sign anything right away. Let me say that once more to be clear about its importance: Do not sign any documents. My guess is that most personal injury lawyers will expect you to sign the fee agreement at that initial meeting. Resist any temptation to do so. Instead, insist on getting back to them. For those who pressure you to sign by using manipulative comments suggesting your case will be disadvantaged if you wait, tell them you must think about hiring them. Add that this is an important decision and you hope they can understand you'll need a day or two to consider hiring them. Avoid answering further questions such as when you'll be getting back to them and which other attorneys you're considering. Ask to take the forms with you to review.

How do you know if you are receiving adequate representation? Most importantly, your lawyer should keep you informed. If you call with a question, he or she should return that call within a reasonable time (one to two days). You should understand that in the case of complicated litigation it would be unreasonable to expect your lawyer to mail you copies of all pleadings or to debrief you on every (or even some) conversations he or she has had with opposing counsel, court officials, or collaterals. You are, however, entitled to reasonable updates. You are also entitled to an explanation of your lawyer's strategy for success, an approximation of the case's duration, and notice of major developments in the case (e.g. important hearings, depositions, major expenses, and any offers of settlement). Anything beyond that would be a bonus and might qualify your lawyer as above-average to exceptional in the communications category.

Your lawyer should be respectful to you. This may seem like a trivial requirement, but as anyone who either is a lawyer or has had significant dealings with them knows—lawyers are often pompous SOBs. Don't let yours talk down to you, disparage your lack of legal knowledge or in any way make you feel uncomfortable. I suppose this approach has its dangers as well, in that many clients disrespect their lawyers. When empowered as 'the boss' they are more inclined to overstep the boundaries which are essential to any effective attorney/client relationship.

Let's run through some examples of attorney disrespect and how you might respond. (You should note that this sampling is based on observations and stories others have shared with me). If your lawyer is accompanying you to court, particularly where a contested hearing is involved, he or she should (out of respect to his paying client) maintain detachment and professionalism. Frequently, I notice lawyers exhibiting too much friendliness to opposing counsel in front of their clients. Please don't misunderstand my point. I'm strongly in favor of camaraderie. I hope you'll agree, though, as to the difference between collegiality and a fifteen minute, jovial, public conversation about one's family or social life. My point is that in the latter instance, your lawyer would be unlikely to take a hard stand on your behalf against his "buddy." Consider the battle comparison: If two five-star generals were sharing war stories in front of their troops and then ordered attacks against each other, would they instill confidence in their soldiers?

If you're being deposed (asked questions under oath as part of a legal proceeding) relative to a case in which you've incurred serious injuries, you should expect tough questions from the insurance company's lawyer. On occasion, you may encounter a lawyer who crosses the border of tough into mean and sleazy. He is intent on breaking you down and perhaps pressuring and twisting your testimony in a fashion which furthers the ends of his billion-dollar corporate client. He may fail to comply with procedural requisites. What are you supposed to do? You're not a lawyer, so you may not know what's appropriate from a procedural standpoint.

That's where your lawyer must be proactive and aggressive in protecting your rights. Again, I'm a fan of conciliation and negotiation. Cooperation is also a good thing. Appeasing volatile behavior is different. If your lawyer attempts appeasement in these circumstances, you should consider terminating him or her. Lawyers should never be neutral. They should and must, within the bounds of the law, be attuned solely to their clients' interests.

Terminating your lawyer in the context of a personal injury case, or any case, is always exclusively your choice. An unhappy lawyer, upon notice of your decision to terminate him or her, may try to manipulate you to think otherwise. That's why, to avoid the pressure or stress of responding to the 'jilted lawyer', it's often best to not go through him.

What am I suggesting here? If you've concluded your dissatisfaction with your lawyer is irreparable, first you should find an acceptable replacement. If your current, incompetent attorney suspicions that you are defecting and initiates a barrage of phone calls to persuade you otherwise, don't respond. You have no obligation to do so, ethically or otherwise.

Once you've secured your new lawyer, he or she should draft a letter to your terminated lawyer, indicating your decision and emphasizing that the terminated lawyer must cease from contacting you in the future.

Don't worry about cushioning your decision. Your terminated lawyer failed to adequately perform and you made a reasonable decision. Move forward and be glad you implemented change before more damage was done.

B. Criminal cases

There's a reason why criminal defendants are appointed counsel. The degree to which their lives and liberty are in jeopardy will vary, depending on the charges. For some, there's a lot a stake, from incarceration to the death penalty. Nonetheless, the often quoted legal truism ("He who represents himself has a fool for a client") is particularly apropos here.

I shake my head whenever I hear of a self-righteous defendant, so sure of his innocence and ability to play lawyer that he refuses the assistance of competent counsel. Jack Kevorkian, the notorious Michigan doctor dubbed "Dr. Death" for his liberal view and implementation of patient-assisted suicides, stood trial for violating the state ban on such procedures. He fired his lawyer, Geoffrey Fieger, in the face of what appeared to be his insatiable ego and blind (as well as destructive) self-righteousness. Mr. Fieger is a rarity in that he is a celebrity lawyer who actually achieves results. Most of the attorney 'experts' you see as regular commentators on CNN and other cable networks are either legal hacks with good PR

PART III

people or inactive listeners.

Anyhow, Dr. Death lost his criminal case. How could he, an intelligent man but with no legal training, compete with the top lawyers in the Michigan DA's office in such a high-profile case? He has never written briefs, argued motions, or the like. He was facing serious charges. What was he thinking? He obviously was not. My guess is arrogance took hold of him, prompting a belief that his crusade would best be served if he went solo. Like many disillusioned pro se litigants, perhaps he felt an attorney would run interference with his direct dialogue with the jury. To the contrary, not having a lawyer looks bad to the jury, particularly if the pro se party has difficulty articulating. More notably, judges dislike pro se advocates. It's burdensome for them to break down commonplace procedures for non lawyers. They're also concerned that an appeals court could reprimand them for failing to protect the Due Process rights of those who don't understand the law as well as lawyers. The trial, with a pro se litigant, becomes twice as long. I've seen this irritate and frustrate many judges. That's why you often see judges urge pro se litigants to get lawyers. They'll repeatedly remind them that they are held, at least in theory, to the same knowledge of procedure as the defendants who have lawyers.

Because of the stakes in criminal cases, all criminal defendants are appointed counsel where hiring their own counsel would represent a financial burden. (For the Trivial Pursuit players reading, the landmark Supreme Court Case which mandated that right was <u>Gideon v. Wainwright</u>). Keep in mind, though, that you are merely entitled to counsel, not a superstar attorney. Court appointed lawyers run the gamut in terms of ability, work ethic, and passion. I read an article in the <u>New York Times</u> documenting how shabby the representation of court-appointed lawyers was. One such attorney fell asleep during a murder trial.

I handle some court-appointed cases in the child custody context and some of my best friends are conscientious, well-prepared court-appointed attorneys. On the flip side, other lawyers don't take these cases as seriously as they would for a client who paid a sizeable retainer. In addition, the state (as opposed to the client) pays your fee, allowing for a bit of disconnect in the attorney-client relationship.

My general advice is therefore to accept the appointment of counsel, particularly where having counsel would be helpful, and paint an appearance of cooperation to the judge. At the same time, be prepared to fire your court-appointed counsel and hire private counsel if you sense your interests are not being adequately protected under the current arrangement. Different circumstances, of course, may dictate a modified course of action. For example, if you have a competent private criminal attorney available (and the requisite resources to pay) it may make sense to hire that lawyer immediately. One piece of advice on hiring private criminal lawyers: don't pay in cash and do insist on a fee agreement. I've heard stories of cash payments, no paper trail and frustrated criminal defendants.

I have a couple more points to make about court-appointed counsel. Obviously, they are free. Things that are free and enticing to the unwary consumer can be dangerous. Humor me for a moment, if you would, with a personal anecdote. Some years ago, my wife and I received a letter from a real estate developer touting a new time-share opportunity. Just for meeting with them, the letter promised, we would receive free round trip airfare. I silenced my suspicions and accompanied my wife that Fall afternoon to the location which was about an hour from our home. Annoyingly, the only thing which was truly free (e.g. without strings) was the stale popcorn. A wired sales rep pestered us with questions and sleazy come-ons, ignoring the main draw—namely the 'free' plane tickets. After forty-five minutes, I queried about the airfare and she detailed the numerous limitations, such as flight schedule, location, etc. In addition, we would be required to sit for other instructive meetings before we qualified. I had heard enough. If I had to see one more piece of popcorn or listen to another word, I would have vomited.

What do time-share gimmicks have in common with court-appointed lawyers? The answer is simple: They support my theory that free offerings often cost more than the things and services you have to pay for. The cost, of course, is not monetary. You will pay in time, shoddy product and (in the frequent case of court-appointed lawyers) representation which jeopardizes your freedom.

The penny pinchers abound, and they are frequently in the wealthiest category of people. I have had multimillionaire clients who protest the $30 to $40 in constable charges to serve legal documents. Clearly, there is a distinction to be recognized between a cheap bastard and a wise, frugal person. The latter category includes individuals whose accumulation of wealth is attributable to their fiscal restraint. Otherwise said, they do not spend money on unnecessary goods and services, and they shop for the best price on items they need. Further, they live below their means and save whatever surplus monies are available.

Wise people would never represent themselves in a criminal matter. They would either find competent appointed counsel or secure a private lawyer who has a reasonable fee structure. What is reasonable? For cases in court, most lawyers request retainers. A retainer is an upfront payment which the lawyer must deposit in his or her client trust account. He bills against the retainer at his hourly rate.

Some lawyers charge flat fees at each stage of the proceedings, but it is unethical for lawyers to charge contingent fees in criminal cases. From a practical standpoint, it makes no sense for a lawyer to condition his fee on the success of the case. There's no 'pot of gold' as there is in an accident case, so the lawyer would have to secure funds from the exonerated defendant. Since it is unlikely the defendant is employed or has any savings, you may have worked for free!

Retainers billed out hourly are the most common

arrangements. As indicated earlier, I have heard of $25,000 and even $50,000 retainers. My view, though, is that you can get a good (possibly exceptional) lawyer for $15,000 or less up front. You should also keep in mind that lawyers may only pay themselves from the retainer (which must be maintained in a separate, interest-bearing account) when they've earned the money. In other words if the lawyer logs three hours on the case, he may pay himself his hourly rate times three hours, and he must provide you with an accounting.

Effective representation in a murder trial, I'm told, may cost tens of thousands of dollars. That sounds like a lot of money to most people; to some it may appear to be too much or a waste if you can get a 'free' lawyer.

Remember though, that money comes and goes. A criminal record is permanent, and I've heard that prison is not fun.

C. Family Law Cases

Massachusetts has elected to facilitate family law cases. That means family courts are people-friendly courts, unlike their counterparts at the state and federal level. The family law clerks, at least those in Boston with whom I am in regular contact, are instructed by their supervisors to work closely with pro se litigants. In fact, the pro se litigants are provided with questionnaires, used to assess the helpfulness of staff. Why pay for a lawyer when the family law system caters to pro se litigants? Further, though they are required to hold non-lawyer litigants to the same standard of competency as lawyers, family court judges rarely abide by that principle. I cannot say for certain what motivates them to cater to pro se litigants. Perhaps it is pressure from court administrators. It could be a unique phenomenon in Massachusetts, given our legacy of liberalism and protection of individual rights.

It reasons that in many family court cases, it makes sense to go without a lawyer. Family courts handle numerous matters in

PART III

addition to divorce cases: paternity (custody disputes in which the parties are not married), guardianships, state intervention (where parental rights may be terminated), modifications, and contempts.

With the exception of the high end divorce matters, which we discussed in the prior section, divorce-type cases generally don't require counsel. Let's take modifications, for example, where one of the parties seeks to change a material provision of an existing judgment. In Massachusetts, that party files a complaint to modify the judgment. For most such complaints, no filing fee is required. Further, Massachusetts has implemented the lawyer-for-a-day program in which attorneys provide free legal advice to pro se litigants. They do not appear in court or sign documents on their behalf. They merely advise. You can inquire at the clerk's office. Like everything, some advice is good, some is less than good. Nonetheless, I believe it is worth listening to these folks.

Returning to our example, when a party seeks to change a material term of a judgment, he or she may obtain the complaint for modification form at the court. With the assistance of the lawyer-of-the-day or court employee, the pro se litigant may hand-write the basis for seeking to modify the existing judgment. He or she can also mark up a motion before the court at the judge's earliest available date. In many instances, no filing fee accompanies these types of complaints, meaning the litigant is only responsible for paying the $40 or $50 for constable service of the summons and complaint.

At the hearing, the judge will modify the judgment upon a showing that the parties' circumstances have substantially changed since the judgment was entered. Most of the modification cases involve child support obligations, with the non-custodial parent seeking to lower the weekly obligation or the custodial parent vying for an increase.

With contempt complaints, we are generally talking about dead-beat dads (who usually come up with back support when facing jail time). In uncontested divorces, assuming that the parties maintain civility throughout the process, they will merely need to fill out forms and appear at a hearing in which a judge approves their divorce agreement. So, in all of the above matters, one would be wise to consider disavailing him or herself of legal counsel.

We must then answer the question of when does one need a lawyer in family law cases? Let's begin here: What I'm about to say won't surprise most people, though one would wish otherwise. Money complicates things, particularly litigation. Otherwise said, money provides a means of over-doing things. At the same time, in my view, the well-funded are not automatically endowed with intelligence or greater humanity. So, you can see what a bad combination this is. Add to the mix a devious, high-priced lawyer and you can readily see why the opposing side should hire his or her own lawyer so as to protect his interests.

If money were not an issue, and I speak as a blunt litigation attorney, a lawyer could spin a legal mess for a pro se opponent. Let me try to illustrate by example in the context of a divorce case. Say the parties have been married for about five years and have two minor children. Further, assume the wife has a lawyer and that the husband does not. After filing the complaint for divorce, the wife's lawyer can file and schedule a motion seeking such things as temporary custody, child support, and alimony. She may compile numerous affidavits from family, friends, neighbors, teachers, medical personnel, etc.

Then you'll be hit with requests for documents. As a non-lawyer you'll be unaware of your rights with respect to objecting. You may produce documents in response to requests which are otherwise impermissible due to their overbroad or invasive nature. In addition, you may provide incomplete answers or documentation, prompting the lawyer to file a motion to compel. Motions for sanctions may follow.

Next, you'll be notified of a series of depositions,

culminating in yours and possibly that of your employer, ex-spouse or significant other, family, neighbor, friend, and enemy. So, you'll be encountering the ire of these individuals whose lives and work schedules are being disrupted on account of your divorce proceedings. 'Strained" would characterize your relationship with these folks. There's also concern as to what they might say during depositions. With a devious lawyer on the other side, you should anticipate he or she will distort facts to obtain statements which portray you in an unfavorable light. Time will also be an issue, since you will need to attend each of the scheduled depositions-some of which may last an entire day.

Your deposition will be a more unpleasant experience. You'll be asked questions aimed at trapping you into partial admissions of your poor parenting, verbal/physical abuse, high earning potential, and the like. As a non-lawyer, you won't know when to object, how to answer, or which questions should be redirected. In short, the lawyer will devour you like a hungry cheetah would a water buffalo.

Do I need to keep going with this example?

Let's move forward to the next category of questions. Having decided to hire a divorce lawyer, your first concern is how to find an appropriate one. Word of mouth works best where the referrer is someone whose opinion you trust. If that option is unavailable, there are bar referral services and Yellow Pages ads. If you are unemployed or have low income, you may qualify for a free lawyer through a local legal services agency. Without re-hashing the Catch-22 nature of this arrangement, I refer you to our earlier discussion.

Interviewing a few divorce lawyer prospects makes sense. I find that people put too much emphasis on experience in the context of matrimonial matters. Simply stated, most lawyers are dispassionate. What you want here is a high level of empathy. That's not to say that you shouldn't prioritize competence. You want someone who has familiarity with the process and who has brought at least a handful of comparable cases to successful resolution.

Selecting a lawyer who believes in your case is always important, though especially so in divorce matters. Why do I think that? These are highly emotional cases. Since judges have so much discretion in rendering decisions, I've noticed the credibility of witnesses magnifies. As an extension of their clients, divorce lawyers are assessed in the same manner; those who lack the compassion to support their clients' emotional contentions negatively affect those cases.

To provide a helpful roadmap, here's a working list of some questions you should ask a prospective divorce lawyer:

1. How long have you been practicing for?
2. Have you recently handled (with success) this type of case?
3. What would your strategy be?
4 What are our chances of achieving my objectives?
5. How do you feel about my case?

I've emphasized the last question, since it will allow you to gauge the empathy of your prospect. Of course, asking the forward question, "Are you compassionate, sensitive, etc.?" is a waste of time for the simple reason that he or she will respond in the affirmative without regard for truthfulness. For that matter, who on earth doesn't consider him or herself to be compassionate or a good, caring person? Body language, tone, eye contact, mood, and the like are far greater responders to the fifth question I've posed.

Unfortunately, we have to address the financial piece. I say 'unfortunately' perhaps because I cringe at the lawyer caricatures our society has painted, as they focus on our perceived value of money over effective representation. The reality is that lawyers should be distrusted in the same way you might be skeptical of the quotes provided by doctors, dentists, electricians, auto

PART III

mechanics, general contractors, and so forth.

That said, what are we talking about here in terms of reasonable fees? Since most divorce lawyers request a retainer before commencing work, you'll need to assess the fairness of the hourly rate and the retainer. I would discourage you from attempting to negotiate the quoted figures, though many people try and lawyers often accommodate these requests. If you don't like the price, don't hire the lawyer. It's not like buying a house or a car where the transaction is readily over. If you pressure or irritate your lawyer by negotiating a lower price, he or she may not commit to your case in the same manner he commits to his other, market-rate-paying clients. Who would you care more about, with all other variables equal, a client paying you two hundred an hour or one paying one hundred fifty and likely complaining about your charges?

The complexity of the case should determine the attorneys' fees. I realize that some lawyers couch behind the mantra of experience to drive up their hourly rates. Granted, a twenty-year divorce attorney will likely perform at a higher level than a rookie lawyer. Notwithstanding that type of extreme comparison, many other factors determine whether your prospective lawyer is best for you. For example, with a younger lawyer you might encounter someone more ambitious and disposed to hard work and client satisfaction. If you feel an intangible connection with the prospective lawyer, to me that's worth more than someone's Harvard pedigree, high profile cases, or purported coziness with local family court judges. The smugness, self-righteousness, and entitlement of some older lawyers astounds me. Don't they get it by now? No one wants to hear their self-serving musings.

I believe a fair hourly rate should range from $175 to $275. On average, a reasonable retainer might be $5,000. The reason why lawyers frequently seek retainers, and I speak from experience, is because of clients' disinclination to pay more once the case begins. Further, after a lawyer has entered an appearance as counsel, it's difficult to withdraw (even if your client's failure to pay is the reason). Contrary to what a layperson might think, a lawyer is ethically inhibited from ending representation in a court case unless successor counsel appears or a judge permits withdrawal.

Please don't misunderstand me, though. As tough as it may often be to run a 'law business', lawyers do not and should not be allowed to bill an unsuspecting or unprepared public. Otherwise said, I am not an apologist for over-billing. You have the right to question your prospective lawyer on fees. If he or she is resistant or provides politician-type responses, you should be leery. Consider that our cities, towns, and states abound with lawyers; don't hesitate to end an interview if things don't feel right.

D. Estate Planning

With the exception of a simple will or health care directive, I believe you should consult a qualified lawyer (and accountant) in planning your estate. Elders should consider protecting assets from the state in the event nursing home care is required, a process known as Medicaid Planning. With both elders and middle-aged folks, nuances abound, meaning that dabbling where tens of thousands to millions of dollars are involved is poor judgment.

Trusts are effective vehicles in tax planning, in achieving flexibility, and as a means of ensuring continuity in the event of injury or incompetence. Yes, the forms are available at office supply stores. Making them suit your needs is a challenging task, best left to a professional. In a nutshell, a trust operates as follows: The creator names a trustee to manage what's in the trust (real estate, money, investments, or some combination thereof) for the benefit of one or more people (the beneficiaries). The creator may also serve as trustee and beneficiary.

Irrevocable trusts may be used by elders to relinquish control of assets, while special needs trusts are crafted to maximize the benefits disabled persons may receive. Most common, though, are relatively straightforward trusts a middle-aged husband and wife create to avoid the time-consuming probate process and to provide for flexibility.

I've handled a fair number of estate and elder planning cases and conclude that consumers need to be particularly careful when it comes to hiring lawyers in these matters. Rip-offs and over-charging run rampant here. Why? Here are some reasons: First, elderly people are more vulnerable and therefore susceptible to exploitation. Second, though geriatric doctors and other medical professionals are often notorious violators in this regard, some elder lawyers should share that reputation.

Attorneys who represent the elderly can sucker unsuspecting victims with their gentle talk, caring manner, and low-key approach. Many of these lawyers exploit elders. I know firms that specialize in this area that charge an elder $500 or more for an initial interview, which is followed by some terse letter of recommendation regarding how they should proceed. Then they might advise a few documents and suggest the law firm serve as trustee of the trust. By the time the financial dust clears, the bill approaches $10,000.

What are some other red flags in dealing with elder lawyers? In addition to the sizeable, initial consultation fee, be wary of a liberal rolodex. If the prospective lawyer is rattling off names of his buddy the financial planner who's "such a good guy" or his close friend the life insurance specialist who "you must see" make your way to the door. You should expect that he has some personal stake in your contacting these collaterals. It may not take the form of a kickback, but if it did then that would be a clear ethical violation. It's more likely that his buddy the financial planner will refer him clients in exchange for his referring you. The better approach, which I do on occasion, is to refer the names of a few professionals in the event the client makes inquiry on the subject.

Another bad sign is if your prospective elder attorney requests a sizeable retainer. With very limited exception, my opinion is that all estate planning matters should be handled on a flat-fee basis. The reason being that unlike with court cases, lawyers can readily determine how many hours they require to prepare estate-planning documents. For example, if a lawyer has a motion hearing scheduled for 9am, he or she may wait for four hours before the case is called or the case may be called promptly at nine. In the former instance, the attorney may need to bill for five hours. Or, as often happens, the case could be continued the next day, too. With travel time and preparation time the lawyer could end up spending 20 hours. Accordingly, charging a flat fee for this type of work is ineffectual and financially risky. Since estate planning merely involves the drafting of documents, time is not as much of a variable and therefore a flat fee makes sense.

A similar reasoning applies to lawyers who are silent, vague or defensive about fees. My approach is to be as open as possible about the subject because, obviously, clients care a great deal about how much they'll be paying. I find that the 'silent' lawyer is the worst because he'll send you an inflated bill after completing your estate planning. Beyond the purview of this discussion, the same advice should apply to your dealings with contractors, plumbers, and other service providers.

Elders should, to the extent possible, have a son, daughter, friend, or trusted advisor accompany them to initial meetings. The purpose is two-fold. On the one hand, it should comfort them to have a caring person with them where stressful issues are discussed. On the other, it will head-off an overly aggressive lawyer. If leaving in the middle of the meeting becomes necessary, it'll be easier to do so with someone else. It doesn't make much sense for me to re-visit the laundry list of questions to ask a prospective elder attorney, where we've addressed them earlier. They apply in equal force here. I will speak to lawyers' fees, though.

PART III

How much should estate-planning cost? Five hundred for an initial meeting, as we discussed, exceeds the bounds of reasonableness. I'll either charge for an hour's time or request a flat fee of $100. Often I'll agree to waive the initial consultation in the event the client hires me for the estate planning work. I've encountered some resistance from prospective clients who feel the initial meeting should not be charged. While I can appreciate the inherent concerns in that position, I must explain to that camp of thinking a number of things. First, I, like most lawyers, don't charge for the initial meeting of contingent cases and even prospective contingent ones. I'll be direct and honest here in revealing that many lawyers don't charge for the initial consultation. Those lawyers though, either limit the initial meeting to fifteen minutes or don't run wise businesses. In response to my request for a consultation fee, these clever prospective clients will attempt to substitute a phone screening for an in-person meeting. I then ask them whether any doctor would or could possibly make a diagnosis of their ailment on the phone. The question is, of course, rhetorical. No sane doctor would ever announce a diagnosis without seeing the patient in person, conducting tests, perhaps reviewing past records, and gathering insurance information for billing purposes. In short, doctors require and charge for an initial consultation before making diagnoses, and so should lawyers.

Second, I receive an average of ten calls per week from prospective new clients. Of those, I'd say I take on one or two as clients. That means eight or nine per week do not become new clients. Were I to gratuitously meet with each of those callers for an hour to an hour and a half, you can see how much time I would ultimately lose each week. Thirdly, in the event I meet with a few prospective clients and they don't hire me, I'll have wasted a few hours if I don't charge. So, I'll quote a flat fee at the time of the initial meeting, though typically I'll have an idea what to charge when I first speak with them on the phone. For a basic estate plan (wills, durable powers of attorney,

THE LAWYER WITHIN

and health care directives for husband and wife) I'll charge about $800. For simple trusts, I might charge around $750.

For a more complicated estate plan, typically where assets approach the million-dollar range, I might charge between $1,500 and $2,000. Unless litigation is involved, I can't think of an occasion where I've set a higher fee.

Keep this in mind if a prospective lawyer wants $10,000 to organize your affairs. Say thank you and leave without further discussion.

E. Intangible Characteristics of Good Lawyers

Our country has approximately one million lawyers, a staggering figure in light of our two hundred sixty-five million people. The latter number, of course, includes children and retirees. I would guess the lawyer ratio among the work force borders one in two hundred.

Where am I going here? My point is that lawyers abound. In my view, though, becoming a lawyer requires some education and intelligence, and a large percentage of my profession lacks one or more of these essential qualities of good lawyers. Therefore, in finding an appropriate lawyer it is helpful to understand characteristics of good lawyers. Your task is to sift through the chaff to find the wheat. Let's talk about the wheat, noting that none of the following requires a law degree. In fact, having one may be a hindrance.

1. Self Esteem:

Distinguish bravado, which runs rampant among lawyers, from healthy confidence. Here comes another moment of bluntness: Attorneys are often negatively perceived for a good reason. Many are deceiving, disingenuous, pompous loud mouths with twisted notions of integrity and fair dealing. These narcissists share a commonality: They ironically suffer from low self-esteem.

PART III

I've said this numerous times and it seems to always hold true. The best, most fearsome lawyers against whom I've ever competed have invariably been centered, somewhat reserved, polite, and professional men and women. Therein, I believe, lies the hallmark of self-esteem. Those who feel good about themselves don't need to bully others or be strident to get what they want. Further, they recognize the inefficiency of such behavior. It alienates court officials, clients, and other collaterals connected to the case, clouds the issues, and wastes energy.

Maybe our society has become comfortable with the stereotype of successful lawyers as selfishly aggressive and immoral. It certainly plays well on television and in the movies. Reality is different. Good judges rarely tolerate, much less enjoy, self-consumed trial lawyers who flout their authority and the rules of procedure.

It follows that in acting as your own lawyer you would be well-served to follow the path of quiet efficiency: Kicking and screaming, pressure tactics, and the like do not work. Feeling good about yourself means maintaining connection and harmony with your environment and fellow constituents.

2. Preparation

As an attorney, I relish the underdog role. I suppose having a small practice puts me in that category by definition. Insurance defense lawyers are paid handsomely and are often equipped with a team of support staff to assist in litigation. Medium and large firms may have three or four lawyers appear in each case. The senior partners might bill at $500/hour.

As a self-advocate, or with representation, you may encounter comparable odds. You may have a trumping advantage though: a superior work ethic. Preparation is the great equalizer, and it is a golden product of hard work.

Cases often turn on the presentation of a single issue or a couple of facts. To the extent you or your counsel knows those facts or that issue much better than your opponent, and if you have analyzed all the possible arguments that he or she may advance, your chances of succeeding compound.

3. Kind Aggressiveness and Toxic People

This phrase may seem like a contradiction in terms, though my view is that each cannot be mutually exclusive in successful advocacy. A kind person is popular among all with whom he has contact, though his popularity may stem from the fact that people can freely take from him what they wish.

At the polar opposite is the 'toe-stepper', whom we've all encountered in some form and, I dare say, of whom we garner some disdain. This person may lack in self-esteem (see earlier discussion) and have attention-deficit issues. Further, this pushy guy or gal may achieve some short term gains, prompting some to buy into the fallacious belief that success hinges on mimicking these behaviors.

Let's break down these short-term gains to expose their weaknesses. I'm going to illustrate those weaknesses by using the example of a mean-spirited insurance lawyer with whom I once dealt. He will remain nameless, but I assure you he is a psycho-analyst's dream. If ever there was a toxic person, he is it.

In a nutshell, I was representing three individuals of high credibility who were injured in a car accident. One of the three owned and drove the car in which the others were passengers. The facts bore out the clear liability of a second vehicle, which illegally left the scene of the accident. The insurance company of my client who was the owner and operator of the first vehicle, under Massachusetts law, was required to pay reasonable medical expenses, within a certain dollar value, of all three individuals. That insurance company, however, could conduct a reasonable inquiry of the facts, including what they call an 'examination under oath' (EUO).

When I received notice from Mr. Toxic of his representation of the insurance company and his client's intention to proceed

PART III

with the EUO, I promptly responded back that I would coordinate available dates for our four respective schedules. One week or so later, he fired a nasty letter to me, threatening to cut off my clients' benefits because I hadn't responded quickly enough for his liking.

As is my protocol in these types of situations, I gave peace one chance, attempting a conciliatory phone call to smooth over any 'misunderstanding'. He didn't answer his line, so I left a message. Two days passed without response, leading me to believe that he was not intent on speaking to me and that I would need to write a gentle letter of clarification.

His response to my neutral letter was an immediate written attack, with more admonitions and demanding a tight, controlled timetable. To cut this long story down, his belligerence and pushiness led to a fight over practically everything. Perhaps he believes his insurance company client will be pleased with his approach. I can't imagine they're enamored with the substantial bill he must have sent them for such unnecessary rancor. In addition, he has alienated me for life and must have raised his blood pressure considerably. He will need to expend more money on personal therapy appointments and medications.

Now let us draw the line between these extremes and define the parameters of what I call 'kind aggressiveness'. It might be helpful to think of it as one part procedure, a second part substance, and a third part common sense. Your procedure or presentation in advocacy must be professional and gentle. If you are curt, obnoxious, or anything like that, most people will push you aside regardless of what you have to say. We are all so eager to be heard and often so consumed with our own agenda that we fail to account for the feelings of the person or people to whom we are seeking to appeal. That is where common sense comes into play.

By presenting with kindness, your audience will soften, affording you the opportunity to inject your substance. Most people appreciate assertiveness and aggressiveness as long as it

THE LAWYER WITHIN

is controlled and not unleashed on them.

If you can master or at least become proficient at this technique, you will rise high above most others who attempt to subjugate with heavy-handedness.

4. Resiliency

Be honest with yourself in answering these questions:

1. Does it take you a long time to process and move beyond criticism and disappointments?
2. Are you a highly sensitive person?
3. Are you a grudge-holder?
4. Do you quit easily?

If you respond affirmatively to more than one, I think you'll need to work on detachment, at least when it comes to acting as your own lawyer. Success in advocacy, I've discovered, is often as much about resiliency (a.k.a. not giving up) as anything else.

Let's back up a moment. No one likes being judged or criticized and those who accuse others of being "thin-skinned" are ironically often afflicted with that very ailment. It's also worth emphasizing that I am an adamant believer in proactive responses to verbal abuse and would be among the last to minimize such conduct or encourage you to make sense of it. You can't and shouldn't try to do so. Bad luck is also something with which you should not become consumed.

I'll concede that some of us have more energy than others, but it's within reason. So let's assume each of us has enough energy to fill a tall cup. If you waste that energy on worrying about past events or future ones, you'll have less, or even none, left.

Effective advocacy requires your full concentration and energy. If you are preoccupied with a disappointing event which occurred yesterday, you risk jeopardizing the task in front of you. Further, if an initial set-back in your legal matter renders you paralyzed in your thoughts and freezes or drains your confidence, your chances of success dwindle.

Wouldn't it be nice to press a button, say a password or imbibe a magic potion to acquire resiliency? Such fantasies, unfortunately, are limited to novels and movies. There are ways in which you can increase your resiliency if you believe it needs work. Let's discuss a few:

a.) Accept that you are the master of your thoughts

As such, you have the power to eliminate those which sap your energy and the ability to forward think. When a judge or magistrate makes an initial ruling against you, it hurts even the most thick-skinned person. Accept life's imperfections and remind yourself that no one strolls through life without blemish. More to the point, all highly successful people have struggled at stages in their lives. In this context, I'm always reminded of my favorite historical figure, Abraham Lincoln. He dealt with business failure, unsuccessful political elections, the loss of a sibling and parent at a young age, the deaths of two of his children, and what was likely his own mental illness and that of his wife. Notwithstanding those traumatic events, each of which could have independently deterred most optimistic folks, Lincoln persevered to achieve the Presidency and preside over our country during its most trying period, becoming (in the opinion of many noted historians) the greatest President ever. What an inspiration!

Practice filling your head with happy, positive thoughts every day and avoid people and things which move your thoughts in the opposite direction.

b.) Unlearn quitting

It is easy to give up, make an excuse, and then point a finger at someone or something else. After all, it is common in our society, even among our most visible constituents (e.g. politicians, actors, and sports figures). Nonetheless, I would submit that those who ascribe to such conduct fail in the long run. Further, quitting feels bad.

Please humor me as I illustrate with a personal example. In high school, I succeeded in track, particularly the 400m race. In college, I expected to achieve the same results, only to discover that the competition was far greater. Accordingly, I had to work twice as hard as most of the other athletes to be competitive. Keep in mind that the workouts were much more rigorous.

There were times when I contemplated quitting and blamed my decision on a lack of natural ability. Many of my friends on the team had done so. Perhaps I was afraid of the isolated feelings a quitter experiences. So, I soldiered through mediocrity for four years, never winning a race or even placing among the top finishers. I did see my times improve and was taught powerful lessons in humility, hard work, and resilience which have served me well as a lawyer and in the business world—where I am blessed with perhaps more natural ability than many of my colleagues.

c.) Grow your self-esteem

Self-esteem and resiliency are directly related. It follows that when you feel good about yourself, you're not as touchy and reactive about criticism, and you tend to spring back from disappointment. The key, then, is to keep your self-esteem flowing and to increase production of this valuable commodity. How is that done?

i.) Balance work and play: Sounds like a cliché, and we're all often too busy to assess this important ratio. Maintaining a healthy involvement in clubs and activities you enjoy is one means to this end. If watching a weekly reality television show makes you laugh, watch it. Feeling good, within reason, is never wasteful.

Burn-out is common to all. Lawyers and effective self-advocates are prone to this condition. To the extent you can introduce frivolity to the seriousness of the law and the exacting

PART III

nature of legal proceedings, you will feel better.

Conversely, too much play will render you unprepared and, I believe, will leave you feeling inadequate. I've noticed a category of people who are able to feign diligence when in fact they are lazy. They put on a sunny face and brag about their many projects. As addressed in earlier sections, finger pointing and laziness are buddies. Accordingly, the under-worker/underachiever may secure short-term gains with his machinations. In the longer term, his enemies and bad reputation will converge in causing his undoing. More significantly, when you work hard, in a sense you feel worthy of success. The opposite holds true as well.

I've noticed loafers and procrastinators, and they have a certain hollowness at their core. They may fool others and even themselves with their antics but I believe such behavior is unhealthy. We all, in my opinion, need to feel decent, honest and hardworking. When we're not, it eats away at us, causing an erosion of our integrity.

ii.) Health: I'll keep this section short, deferring to the medical experts and nutritionists who churn out books and lecture regularly on the subject. Let me be more direct and reveal what you already know:

I am not an expert on the topic.

That disclaimer aside, I believe I would be remiss in avoiding these important matters altogether. Let's start with diet. You need not be a nutrition expert to appreciate the correlation between eating well and performing at a high level. Whenever I eat greasy foods, like French fries, I get stomach pains. This physical response may be triggered by my thoughts, to some degree. Alternatively, when I fill my body with fresh fruits, yogurt, grains, and other healthy foods, I feel a natural boost.

My maternal grandfather lived well into his nineties without financial advantage. His secret? Genetics must have played some part. But I think diet was more connected to his longevity. I remember staying with my grandmother and him at their small one-bedroom apartment in Queens. He would eat raw vegetables and garlic, shunning fried foods and meat altogether. In an age of vitamins, pills, and doctors, he took a different path—avoiding all three.

My loving grandpa was also a gentleman, possessor of a warm sense of humor, and someone who ingratiated people. His easy and peaceful nature, I believe, also contributed to this longevity. You may wonder how in a field as contentious as law, one can avoid confrontation. The answer: You can't. On a larger level, those seeking to avoid stress in their lives are disillusioned. You can't do that either. Let's draw an important distinction between avoiding stress and confrontation and monitoring your responses to them. The latter accepts the existence of stress and confrontation, yet seeks healthy means of conflict resolution. The cantankerous bully infrequently runs his blood pressure to a point which compromises his ability to properly function.

If you don't currently exercise, I believe you should reconsider some form of physical activity. Working out serves many beneficial functions in life and, more particularly, in the high-pressure world of law. For one, exercising removes you from stressful thoughts by focusing you on the vigorous task at hand. Additionally, regular workouts strengthen your heart, cardiovascular system and other vital organs, thereby reducing your probability of contracting diseases or illnesses.

When I work out, I feel energized, particularly if I exercise earlier in the morning when most people are just waking up. Yes, it's tough to rally your body at that hour, but the dividends make it worthwhile.

iii.) Loving Yourself and Others: What does a trial lawyer, or any lawyer for that matter, know about love? I will concede that it is easy to believe that most lawyers are heartless. You would base this conclusion, of course, on what you read in the newspaper and see on TV. Many attorneys who appear in those mediums come across in this fashion. Maybe their manifested anger arises from the serious issues in which they are involved. Maybe the cameras and the ego gratification give them a false sense of invincibility. I don't really know.

Well, I believe a highly successful lawyer or pro se advocate must espouse a loving approach with respect to him/herself and others. Sound silly? It isn't. Consider this: When you love yourself, you feel good most of the time and nurture your mind and body. A loving person values and supports others because he wants to share the magic, feel-good potion he's discovered. Giving love grows your sense of security and, in turn, breeds feelings of self-confidence and self-satisfaction.

d.) Simplicity

Keep your thoughts and words, both oral and written, as simple as possible. This will be difficult in light of the fact that our laws were created, it often appears, to confuse. Most judges, clerks, and laypeople appreciate those who can control themselves verbally and who speak in clear, crisp sentences.

You may hear many lawyers speak in a language which seems foreign because it has so many complicated words in it that everyday people don't use. Arrogance and entitlement exacerbate this problem. Don't think that this approach works. It alienates more people than it impresses.

I've noticed a certain presumption which burdens many pro se litigants. They represent themselves for the wrong reasons. To them, the legal process is a sounding board and every time they enter a courtroom, they believe that their Due Process rights hinge on complete deference to whatever they have to say.

How do you keep things simple in legal matters when you're a pro se advocate?

i.) Practice the Two-to-One Rule. Listen to others twice as much as you talk. You will empower people who may become your allies and you will avoid over-speaking. Exercise restraint when the urge arises within you to speak and speak and speak. Avoid unsolicited advice and strong opinions (unless requested).

One can get a rush from feeling omniscient, pontificating and thrusting his opinions onto others. In addition to irritating others with this style, you will greatly increase your sense of stress and responsibility. Consider this example: Your sister comes to you with some concerns about a current boyfriend. She likes him, but doesn't exactly know how to read his behavior and wants to share those thoughts with you.

Let's also assume that you have some strong opinions about the guy, namely you can't stand him. So you're tempted to say so in the hopes she'll wise up and eliminate him from her (and your) life, right?

Here's the catch: She may be complaining not because she wants your endorsement in her quest to dump him, but rather because she is unsure of her feelings and needs your support. If you argue too strongly and loudly, you risk pushing her in the opposite direction. Then, if they reconcile she'll remember you as the one who tried to derail him. Where's the connection to self-lawyering? I'll explain by example: If you appear before a judge, magistrate, or hearing officer, you'll jeopardize the success of your position by failing to listen to and study that person. If you blabber away, it will feel good at the moment. You'll cite some case you researched or ramp up the Bill of Rights, etc. But that self-aggrandizing approach is flawed for the reasons we have discussed.

ii.) Meditation/Awareness Practice. Who has the time to waste on such frivolity, right? Anyone who's practiced meditation in some form or tried related techniques knows its' value is premium. The great thing about it, in my mind, is the ease with which you can become proficient. The only requirements are patience and a small amount of repetition.

In its' basic form, here's how you can maximize the benefits of meditation: During the course of your high-paced day, carve out fifteen minutes. Sit in a chair by yourself in a quiet room. No noises or distractions can co-exist (e.g. radio, television, friends, etc.). That's the easy part. The bigger challenge confronts you once you've created the peaceful environment.

When you sit down, there will be a tendency to reflect on the day's events or to worry about what awaits you in the days, weeks, or months ahead. You must resist that impulse. Otherwise, you will undercut the essence of meditation-namely to let go of all stresses and concerns in your life. Instead, focus on one thing. It can be a number, a word, a person, etc. It should represent a neutral idea. I use the number one. When I'm sitting still, I repeat that word and feel my slow breathing. Typically within minutes my body will relax. It's hard to describe the feeling beyond that, but it's energizing. I'm happy and comfortable. Creative thoughts flow in my mind. I feel confident, healthy, and empowered. Ten to fifteen minutes should be sufficient.

I try to repeat the meditation process up to three times per day, depending on my schedule. The other thing to consider is that effective meditation does not require a perfect environment. In other words, once you've mastered the techniques you should be able to achieve this beneficial, peaceful state in most environments. For example, if you're taking public transportation to work, close your eyes and focus on one word. There may be various noises, making your task more challenging. Keep your focus until you achieve the meditative state.

Awareness techniques (e.g. Zen, yoga, etc.) work similarly. The keys are equanimity and simplicity. If you're interested, you should speak with a specialist, join a class, read a book, etc. Most lawyers and pro se litigants readily disregard this advice.

A final recommendation concerns resting. If my schedule permits, I'll close my door for one half hour every day to take a nap. Typically, I'll recline my chair and sleep. Some people may find more comfort in lying on a mat. Make sure you disable your phone and prevent other interruptions. You'll be amazed how one half hour of rest will re-energize you.

F. A Few Words on Judges

The Founders premised our Constitution on liberty, democracy, and anti-tyranny, though when it comes to the role of judges in the judicial system, I have concerns. In Massachusetts, as with most states and the Federal system, judges are appointed by the executive and tenured immediately. They can only be removed for significant cause. In my fourteen years of practice, I have only known one case of a judge's removal.

You may sense where I am going with this thought. If not, please indulge me. Is it not human nature for one to take certain liberties, assume certain comforts and perhaps exhibit an air of entitlement where one has an unchallenged power to do so? If you knew that your occasional rudeness, laziness, and bias could be tolerated—in fact repeated with impunity—would you be as motivated to be fair, diligent, and impartial? Add the fact that judges are political appointees, and you'll note a system susceptible to abuse.

One of my next projects will be lobbying our state legislature to require judges be voted into office. The detractors say it will politicize the process. Isn't it politicized already, though, if judges are appointed by the Governor? Are we so naïve to believe the Governor will not be inclined to appoint people loyal to and aligned with his political ideology? They also contend the most capable and qualified folks will not seek judgeships if they risk being voted out of office. This is untrue. The current salary schedule of Massachusetts judges, which ranks among the lowest of all states, is a much larger deterrent. If the terms were six or eight years and the pay were fair, there would be no shortage of qualified applicants.

I realize I'm moving in a tangent, but let's finish the point.

PART III

The prospect of being voted out of office would humble the haughtiest of judges, ensuring a level of accountability which lacks in the appointment system. How many judges would roll their eyes, an ugly phenomenon which I've seen numerous times, at lawyers and pro se litigants? Don't you think they'd be more conscientious, thoughtful, diligent? Of course, of course, and of course.

Let's return to the initial discussion. My prior ramblings, at least to this point, represent hopeful thinking. The reality, in Massachusetts and most other states, is that judges are appointed and maintain an entitlement. How do you handle yourself when appearing before a judge? That's the key question. The answer, I believe, must vary depending upon which judge before whom you are appearing. Judges are not robots, devoid of influence, disposition, and temperament.

It follows that you must speak the language of the judge to whom you are speaking. Do some research on his/her background and prior decisions. Watch him/her in court on a day other than when your hearing is scheduled. Does he/she like to talk or ask questions? What seems to make him/her interested or annoyed? I'm amazed by the number of lawyers who think they're Lincoln at Gettysburg each time they're in court. They pontificate and beam, expecting the judge will be awed by their oration. In reality, of course, they frustrate and exasperate even the most patient of judges. Analyze your judge and prepare as you would if you were engaging in negotiations.

FINAL THOUGHTS

One of my life's ambitions is to master the practical. Maybe 'master' is too strong; I'd settle for proficiency. I might begin with basic carpentry skills. How rewarding it would be if I could re-do my kitchen or bathroom without incurring the cost, both financial and mental, of dealing with home improvement contractors.

Next, I'd study nutrition. Everyone knows basic concepts, but I'd like to learn nuances. Herbal sickness remedies and vitamins are two areas which interest me. I'm amazed by the number of products which line the shelves in vitamin stores.

Cooking also fascinates me, as do computers and the stock market.

It seems to me that the downside of our informational and technological advances is that we've become less independent and more beholden to the 'expert' we can secure by pushing a button. We've lost interest in our ability to solve problems autonomously.

That's unfortunate on many levels, the obvious and above-mentioned cost being one of them. Think of self-confidence and happiness, though. Doing things on your own feels good, doesn't it? You're advancing yourself intellectually, emotionally, and spiritually. Also, don't forget that when you do something for yourself, you'll care a lot more about the quality than would the third party you hired to do the project.

I suppose you could say my spirit of individuality, independence, and support of the underdog have motivated me to write *The Lawyer Within*. There's an unfortunate perception, true to a large degree, that money wins cases. Otherwise said, those with money can secure expensive and capable counsel.

As we've discussed, there are many types of cases and legal matters which are best serviced by a qualified lawyer. Through due diligence, you will find a reasonably-priced lawyer with whom you are comfortable.

There are, in equal if not greater force, many opportunities for you to successfully represent yourself. I understand that Hollywood glamorizes and perhaps over-complicates the work of lawyers in a way that intimidates lay people. Otherwise said, some people would never conceive of representing themselves because of their misperception of what it entails. With some common sense, a calm demeanor, persistence, and self-confidence (qualities which are attributable to most successful endeavors) much can be achieved.

One key, I believe, is to establish a mind-set between panic and careless arrogance. In other words, don't be spooked or fearful of the legal process in which you are entangled. At the same time, if you strut into your administrative hearing with sunglasses and cowboy boots, you'll also embarrass yourself.

The other important thing is to know your limits. Representing yourself in certain cases can be hazardous.

There you have it! Let instinct be your guide and self-determination your mantra as you negotiate your way through the legal system. Never underestimate your power to persuade and effect your legal objective: Your Lawyer Within!

APPENDIX

1. <u>CIVIL COMPLAINT</u>

COMMONWEALTH OF MASSACHUSETTS
HAPPY COUNTY, SS.   SUPERIOR COURT DEPT.
                     CIVIL ACTION NO. ___09879___

TINKERBELL Plaintiff, v. PETER PAN, Defendant	)))))))))

<u>PLAINTIFF'S VERIFIED COMPLAINT</u>
<u>with APPLICATION FOR PRELIMINARY INJUNCTION</u>

Now comes the plaintiff, TINKERBELL, ("Plaintiff") through her attorney Jeremy T. Robin and hereby complains against the defendant, PETER PAN ("Defendant") as follows:

<u>Introduction</u>

1. The plaintiff is a natural person, currently residing at 28 Serenity Road, Land of Make Believe.
2. The defendant is an individual, whose address is believed to be 233 Highlight Hills, Playville.
3. This is a case for injunctive relief to enjoin the defendant from foreclosing on the real estate which forms the basis of this complaint, 28 Serenity Road, Land of Make Believe.

<u>Facts</u>

4. The plaintiff repeats and incorporates herein by reference paragraphs 1-3 above.
5. In approximately 1997, the plaintiff purchased the property, which is a three-family house. The plaintiff secured a mortgage with Tom Thumb.
6. At some time thereafter, the plaintiff refinanced her mortgage with Big Bird, Inc. in the approximate amount of $495 thousand.
7. The plaintiff fell behind in her monthly mortgage payments.
8. On or about February 15, 2006, the plaintiff signed a forbearance agreement (<u>See</u> Exhibit 'A'), which set forth a schedule of payments to make up the arrearage and reinstate the original mortgage. The agreement provides that if

	the plaintiff is delinquent on any payment, the defendant has the right to immediate foreclosure.
9.	The plaintiff made timely payments in April and May of 2006.
10.	The plaintiff did not make payments in June and July of 2006.
11.	The defendant, through its agent Oscar the Grouch, opted <u>not</u> to foreclose on the property. The plaintiff spoke with Oscar the Grouch and was assured that if she paid $12,227 by August 27, 2006 (See Exhibit 'B'), the forbearance agreement would be reinstated.
12.	The plaintiff told Oscar the Grouch that she was only able to pay $10,474.69 by August 27. Oscar the Grouch assured her that this figure was acceptable.
13.	On August 27, by Western Union, the plaintiff made payments to the defendant which totaled $10,474.69.
14.	Oscar the Grouch informed the plaintiff that since the payments were not received by 5pm Pacific Standard Time that the defendant would foreclose on the property.

Count I: Breach of Contract/Promissory Estoppel

15.	The plaintiff repeats and incorporates herein by reference paragraphs 1-14 above.
16.	The parties either made an enforceable verbal agreement in which the defendant promised to forbear on foreclosing on the property if the plaintiff paid the sum of $10,474.69 or the plaintiff relied on the defendant's promise to forbear if payment of $10,474.69 was paid and said reliance was to the plaintiff's detriment.
17.	While the plaintiff fulfilled her promise, the defendant has failed to honor its promise of forbearance.

WHEREFORE, Plaintiff prays:

a.	That an Order of Notice issue to the defendant;
b.	Upon return of the Order of Notice that the court restrain and order the defendant to stop any foreclosure proceedings and/or sale of the property and restore the forbearance agreement;
c.	That said action by the Court endure until this matter is set for trial;
d.	That this Court award damages for the defendant's breach of contract; and
e.	For such other and further injunctive relief as the Court deems just and appropriate.

Plaintiff demands a jury trial, pursuant to GL c. 231, section 103.

Plaintiff's Verification

All of the allegations in this complaint are true to the best of my knowledge and belief and I sign under the pains and penalties of perjury.

_____
Plaintiff

                                                Respectfully submitted,
                                                PLAINTIFF
                                                By her attorney,

                                                _____

                                                Jeremy T. Robin
                                                15 Court Square
                                                Boston, MA 02108
                                                (617) 227-0838
                                                BBO #629107

                                                Dated:

2. ANSWER TO COMPLAINT

STATE OF NIRVANA

SUPERIOR COURT DEPARTMENT
CIVIL ACTION NO. 06-22187

Thomas The Tank Engine, *Plaintiff*	} } }
v.	} }
Diesel, *Defendant*	} } } }

DEFENDANT's ANSWER TO COMPLAINT

I. ANSWER TO PLAINTIFF'S COMPLAINT

1. Admit.
2. Admit.
3. Deny.
4. Admit.
5. Deny.
6. Deny.
7. Admit
8. Deny.
9. Defendant can neither admit nor deny

II. AFFIRMATIVE DEFENSES

In further answering the complaint, the Defendant asserts the following affirmative defenses against the claims made by the plaintiff.

FIRST AFFIRMATIVE DEFENSE

The Defendant states that, pursuant to General Laws Chapter 6721(b), the plaintiff has filed a frivolous complaint against him and that the plaintiff should pay all legal fees, expenses, and damages incurred there-from.

SECOND AFFIRMATIVE DEFENSE

The Defendant states that the plaintiff's complaint fails to state a claim upon which relief can be granted. Therefore the complaint should be dismissed.

THIRD AFFIRMATIVE DEFENSE

The Defendant states that to the extent he owed the plaintiffs any duty, he has performed the same.

FOURTH AFFIRMATIVE DEFENSE

The Defendant states that the plaintiff, through his conduct and actions, waived his rights, if any, to the relief sought.

FIFTH AFFIRMATIVE DEFENSE

The Defendant states that the allegations in the plaintiff's complaint resulted from comparative and/or contributory negligence and/or acts or failure to act of a party or parties for whose negligence or acts or failure to act the Defendant is not responsible.

SIXTH AFFIRMATIVE DEFENSE

The Defendant states that to the extent he has any obligations at common law with respect to the rights at issue, he has fully performed his obligations.

WHEREFORE, the Defendant respectfully requests this Honorable Court:

(1) Dismiss the Complaint;
(2) Award the Defendant his reasonable attorneys' fees and costs, and
(3) Grant such other and further relief this Court deems just.

Respectfully submitted,
Diesel,
By his Attorney

Jeremy T. Robin
15 Court Square
Boston, MA 02108
(617)227-0838
BBO 629107

CERTIFICATE OF SERVICE

I, Jeremy T. Robin, attorney for the defendant, do hereby certify that on this day I served a copy of the above document on the following by first class mail, postage prepaid to the plaintiff's counsel:
Thomas The Tank Engine's Lawyer
Tidmouth Station
Island of Sodor

———————————
Jeremy T. Robin

3. <u>INTERROGATORIES</u>

COMMONWEALTH OF MASSACHUSETTS

SUFFOLK, SS. SUPERIOR COURT DEPARTMENT
CIVIL ACTION NO. 87888

SUE JONES, *Plaintiff* v. JOHN SMITH, *Defendant*	} } } } } } } }

DEFENDANT's INTERROGATORIES TO PLAINTIFF

I. Interrogatories

1. Please identify the individual answering these interrogatories. Please include name, address, and a description of employment position.

2. Please identify the terms of your lease with the defendant and how long you have lived in the premises.

3. Identify each and every verbal and/or written complaint you have made to the defendant since the inception of your tenancy with respect to bad conditions and/or items requiring repair in your unit.

4. Identify each and every verbal and/or written complaint you have made to the defendant since the inception of your tenancy with respect to the wooden gate on the 2nd floor landing near the interior stairs located at the premises.

5. Have you ever withheld rent or contacted the Inspectional Services Department regarding conditions in your unit or the common area of the premises? If so, identify the date and/or the other particulars.

6. Please describe, in as much detail as possible, how you allegedly injured yourself on MARCH 11, 2004.

7. Please identify any individuals who witnessed you allegedly injuring yourself on MARCH 11, 2004.

8. Please describe how you came to leave the premises and seek medical care following your alleged incident of MARCH 11, 2004.

9. Please identify each and every medical facility and/or doctor that has provided medical treatment to you for your alleged injuries from the alleged incident of MARCH 11, 2004. Please include in your response dates of service and approximate cost of services.

10. Please identify each and every medical facility that has provided medical treatment to you for back or neck injuries in the past 3 years.

11. Please identify all claims for personal injuries and/or lawsuits for personal injuries you have commenced within the past 5 years.

12. Please identify all lost wages you have incurred from your alleged injuries relative to your alleged accident of August 11, 2006.

13. Please identify all individuals with whom you have shared the particulars of your alleged injuries and/or incident of MARCH 11, 2004.

14. With respect to Interrogatory No. 13, identify the substance of all such conversations.

15. Please identify the approximate date upon which you first notified the defendant of the alleged incident of MARCH 11, 2004 and/or your injuries.

16. Please describe the substance of any conversations with the defendant with respect to the MARCH 11, 2004 incident.

17. Please identify the extent of your anticipated future medical expenses with respect to the alleged MARCH 11, 2004 incident.

18. With respect to each expert witness you intend to call at trial, please identify:
a. the name of each such expert;
b. the subject matter upon which each such expert is expected to testify; and
c. the substance of the facts and opinions of the expert's testimony and the basis of said opinions.

Respectfully submitted,
DEFENDANT,
By his Attorney

_____
Jeremy T. Robin
15 Court Square
Boston, MA 02108
(617)227-0838
BBO 629107

CERTIFICATE OF SERVICE

I, Jeremy T. Robin, attorney for the defendant, do hereby certify that on this day I served the above document on the following by first class mail, postage prepaid to the plaintiff's counsel:

Slick Sammy
35 Dirtbag Way
Reno, Nevada

_____

Jeremy T. Robin

4. DEPOSITION NOTICE

COMMONWEALTH OF MASSACHUSETTS
SUFFOLK, SS.   SUPERIOR COURT DEPT.
                                CIVIL ACTION NO. 087767

Litigation Larry	)
Plaintiff,	)
v.	)
Igor the Instigator	)
Defendant	)
	)

Notice of Taking Deposition

To: Sue Smith, Esq.
      Smith & Thompkins
      84 Trail Road
      Boston, MA 02114

Please take notice that pursuant to Rule 30 of the Massachusetts Rules of Civil Procedure, the Plaintiff will take the deposition upon oral examination of <u>Igor the Instigator</u>, before a Notary Public for the Commonwealth of Massachusetts or some other officer authorized by law to administer oaths at the office of Jeremy T. Robin, 15 Court Square, Suite 200, Boston, MA <u>on FRIDAY MAY 25, 2007, commencing at 9AM</u>. You are invited to attend and cross-examine.

                                                    Respectfully submitted,
                                                    Plaintiff
                                                    By his attorney,

                                                    Jeremy T. Robin
                                                    15 Court Square
                                                    Boston, MA 02108
                                                    (617) 227-0838
                                                    BBO #629107

CERTIFICATE OF SERVICE

I, Jeremy T. Robin, attorney for the plaintiff, do hereby certify that on this day I served a copy of the above document on defendant's counsel of record to the following:
      Sue Smith, Esq.
      84 Trail Road
      Boston, MA 02114

Jeremy T. Robin

5.   CONSUMER DEMAND LETTER

January 12, 2009

Jimmy Stitches
Owner
Quick Buck Cars
525 Freeway Street
Lynn, MA 01905

RE: Bugs Bunny v. Quick Buck Cars
Demand Pursuant to Massachusetts General Laws c. 93A

Dear Mr. Stitches:

This firm represents Bugs Bunny ("Bugs") in conjunction with her claim against Quick Buck Cars ("Quick Buck") for damages pursuant to Massachusetts General Laws, Chapter 93A, Section 9 ("The Consumer Protection Statute").

As you'll note from the purchase agreement I've attached, in February of 2008, Bugs' now-deceased husband purchased a 2003 Lincoln Continental. Though Bugs' name appears as the purchaser, she was not present when the form was signed. Moreover, Mr. Bunny without permission or consent signed her name. The similarity of the signatures, contrasted with Bugs' signature as it appears on a copy of her enclosed Massachusetts Identification Card, proves Mr. Bunny signed her name. You'll note that it is not a drivers' license, because Bugs does not even drive a motor vehicle.

It is unclear exactly what role your staff played when Mr. Bunny forged Bugs' name, except that he/she/they enabled the illegal transaction. Consequently, Bugs' now stands responsible from Sunrise International, the bank which financed the transaction, for the balance of the loan.

By permitting Mr. Bunny to forge Bugs' name as a co-purchaser of said motor vehicle, in order to consummate the sale, Quick Buck engaged in unfair and/or deceptive acts and practices, proscribed under G.L. c. 93A.

Demand is hereby made against Quick Buck as follows:

1. Pay all damages incurred as a result of your Consumer Protection Act violations ($19,356 (the purchase price of said vehicle));
2. Pay Bugs' reasonable attorneys' fees ($1000).

As you should be aware, under the Consumer Protection Act, you are required to respond within 30 days and make a reasonable offer of settlement. Should you fail to do so, a judge may award triple damages, attorneys' fees, interests and costs.

We look forward to your response.

Very truly yours,

Jeremy T. Robin

6. RESIDENTIAL LEASE

STANDARD FORM APARTMENT LEASE
(Executed in Duplicate)

("Lessor") hereby leases to _____ ("Lessee") the following unit ("the premises"): _____. The premises is a 1 bedroom, 1 bathroom condominium unit in a professionally-managed building, including the following fixtures: dishwasher, microwave, and oven. There are coin-operated washers/dryers on the 2nd, 3rd, 4th, and 5th floors of the building. The Lessor has access to all of the washers/dryers, but they are not owned nor are they serviced by the Lessor. The Lessor is also not responsible for the maintenance of the building elevator. The small unit storage space on the 4th floor is <u>not</u> included in the lease.

Lessee shall rent the premises for the term of , beginning and ending. The term rent shall be ____, payable in monthly installments of $ per month (on the first of every month, beginning 9/1/07 since Lessee is paying $ and $ today for Aug. and half of July, respectively). Lessee shall also make a security deposit payment of $ at the inception of the tenancy which Lessor shall deposit in an interest bearing account and otherwise comply with the Massachusetts Security Deposit Statute.

<u>Lessor and Lessee Further Covenant and Agree</u>

1. <u>Care of the Premises</u>: The Lessee shall not paint, decorate, or otherwise embellish and/or change and shall not make nor suffer any additions or alterations to be made in or to the premises without the prior written consent of the Lessor, nor make nor suffer any waste, nor suffer the heat or water to be wasted, and at the termination of this lease shall deliver up the leased premises and all property belonging to the Lessor in good, clean, and tenantable order and condition, reasonable wear and tear excepted.

2. <u>Cleanliness</u>: The Lessee shall maintain the leased premises in a clean condition. He/she shall not sweep, throw, or dispose of, nor permit to be swept, thrown or disposed of, from said premises nor from any doors, windows, balconies, porches or other parts of said building, any dirt, waste, rubbish or other substance or article into any other parts of said building or the land adjacent thereto, except in proper receptacles.

3. <u>Definitions:</u> The words 'Lessor' and 'Lessee' as used herein shall include their respective heirs, executors, administrators, successors, representatives, and assigns, agents and servants. If more than one party signs as Lessee hereunder, the covenants, conditions and agreements herein of the Lessee shall be the joint and several obligations of each party.

4. Disturbance: The Lessee shall not make any disturbing noises in the building nor permit the making of any such noises therein by his family, friends, relatives, invitees, visitors, agents or servants; nor do, nor permit anything to be done by such persons that will interfere with the rights, comforts or conveniences of other occupants in the building. No electric or automatic washing machine, television or other aerials, or other like equipment shall be installed without written consent from the Lessor. No Lessee shall play upon, nor suffer to be played upon, nor operate any musical instrument, radio, television or other like device in the leased premises in a manner offensive to other occupants of the building, nor between the hours of eleven o'clock pm and the following eight o'clock am. Should Lessee be assessed a fine for such disturbance by the condo trustees, he/she shall be solely responsible for paying it and failure to do so will be a material breach of this Lease, entitling the Lessor to commence eviction proceedings.

5. Halls: No receptacles, vehicles, baby carriages or other articles or obstructions shall be placed in the halls or other common areas or passageways.

6. Heat and Hot Water: Pursuant to the Condo Trust Rules, the Lessor pays a monthly fee which covers maintenance of the building's common area, hot water, and head in the common areas. Lessee is solely responsible for heat in the premises and must independently contact the electric company to begin an account and must pay all electric bills.

7. Insurance: Lessee understands and agrees that it shall be Lessee's own obligation to insure her personal belongings. Lessor is not responsible for any lost and/or stolen items or damage to Lessee's property in the premises.

8. Keys and Locks: Upon expiration or termination of the lease, the Lessee shall deliver the keys of the premises to the landlord. Delivery of keys by the Lessee to the Lessor or to anyone on his behalf shall not constitute a surrender or acceptance of surrender of the leased premises unless so stipulated in writing by the Lessor. Locks shall not be changed, altered or replaced nor shall new locks be added by the Lessee without the written permission of the Lessor.

9. Loss or Damage: The Lessee agrees to indemnify and hold the Lessor harmless from all liability, loss or damage arising from any nuisance made or suffered on the leased premises by the Lessee, his family, friends, relatives, invitees, visitors, agents or servants or from any carelessness, neglect or improper conduct of any of such persons. All personal property in any part of the building within the control of the Lessee shall be at the sole risk of the Lessee. The Lessor shall not be liable for damage to or loss of property of any kind due to fire, water, steam, defective refrigeration, elevators or otherwise while on the premises.

10. Parking: This lease does **not** include a parking spot.

11. Storage: This lease does not include storage space outside of the premises.

12. Pets: No pets of any kind are to be kept on the premises at any time (including but not limited to dogs, cats, birds, etc.) without the Lessor's written consent.

13. Repairs: Lessor will at all times keep and maintain the premises and all pipes, wires, glass, plumbing and other equipment and fixtures therein in good repair, order and condition. Should repairs be required, Lessee agrees to contact Lessor and permit a reasonable time to accomplish the repairs and access to the unit.

14. Right of Entry: The Lessor may enter upon the premises for repair purposes, in case of emergency, or to show the premises to prospective purchasers or tenants.

15. Subletting: The Lessee shall not assign nor sublet any part or the whole of the leased premises nor permit any other person or persons to occupy the same absent the written assent of the Lessor.

16. Move-In Fee: Pursuant to the Condo Rules, Lessee agrees to pay a move-in fee of $100.

17. Smoking: Smoking is prohibited at all times either in the premises or in the building. Tenant is responsible for any fine which may be imposed by the condo association for violation of this provision.

18. Rental Payments: Lessee will pay rent, which must be received by the Lessor on or before the 1st day of each month, by check or money order mailed to:

The Lessor's phone numbers are:

19. Bounced checks/Attorneys' Fees for eviction proceedings, notices to quit: Should the Lessee bounce a rent check, a processing fee of $25 must be paid forthwith. Should the Lessor incur any expenses, attorneys' fees or otherwise, due to late payment, nonpayment, or violation of any provision in this lease, the Lessee shall be responsible for such expenses.

Lessor   Lessee

Dated:

7. PURCHASE AND SALE AGREEMENT

PURCHASE & SALE AGREEMENT
(15 Champ Street, Dorchester, MA 02124)

1. PARTIES: Agreement made this day of February, 2006, between Junior Small, hereinafter called the Seller and Will Brandy, hereinafter called the Buyer, as follows:

2. DESCRIPTION: The Seller hereby agrees to sell and the Buyer hereby agrees to purchase upon the terms hereinafter set forth, the following described premises: the property known and numbered as 15 Champ Street, Dorchester, MA 02124

3. BUILDINGS, STRUCTURES, IMPROVEMENTS AND FIXTURES: Included in this sale as a part of said premises are the buildings, structures and improvements now thereon and the fixtures belonging to the seller and used in connection herein, including if any all furnaces, heaters, oil and gas burners and refrigerators, kitchen ranges, mantels, electric and other lighting fixtures, screens, screen doors, storm or other detached windows and doors, blinds, awnings, bathroom fixtures, television antennas, fences, gates, and shrubs.

4. TITLE DEED: Said premises are to be conveyed on or before March 15, 2006 by a good and sufficient Quitclaim Deed of the Seller conveying a good record, clear and marketable title to the same, free of all encumbrances except:
    a. Provisions of local zoning laws, if any;
    b. Existing rights created by instrument of record in party of partition walls (if any);
    c. Taxes for the current year as are not due and payable on the date of the delivery of such deed, and any liens for municipal betterments assessed after the date of this Agreement;
    d. Subject to and with the benefit of any easements, rights of way, covenants, encumbrances and restrictions of record insofar as the same are now in force and applicable and do not interfere with the use of the premises as a three family dwelling.

5. PLANS: If said deed refers to a plan necessary to be recorded therewith the seller shall deliver such plan with the deed in form adequate for recording or registration.

6. PURCHASE PRICE: The agreed purchase price for said premises is $545,000, to be paid as follows: $5,000 as a deposit on this day (to be held by Seller in

a separate escrow account); $540,000 to be paid at the time of delivery of the deed in cash, or by certified, cashier's, treasurer's or bank check or attorney's conveying check.

7. TIME FOR DELIVERY OF DEED: The deed is to be delivered and the consideration paid at the Suffolk Registry of Deeds on March 15, 2006 at 2pm unless some other place and time should be mutually agreed-upon.

8. FINANCING: In order to help finance the acquisition of said premises, Buyer shall apply for an FHA institutional mortgage loan, of $517,750, payable in no less than 30 years at an interest rate not to exceed prevailing interest rates. If, despite the Buyer's diligent efforts, a commitment for such loan cannot be obtained on or before March 1, 2006, the Buyer may terminate this Agreement by written notice to the Seller or Seller's attorney on or prior to said date, whereupon any payments made under this Agreement shall be forthwith refunded and all other obligations of the parties hereto shall cease, and this Agreement shall be null and void without recourse to the parties hereto. Buyer represents that Buyer has already submitted a complete mortgage loan application conforming to the foregoing provisions. Any points charged by the bank are to be paid for by the Buyer. If Seller or Seller's Attorney are not so notified by said date, then failure to obtain financing shall have no effect and Buyer shall be obligated to proceed with this sale. In no event will Buyer be deemed to have used diligent efforts to obtain such commitment unless Buyer submits a complete mortgage loan application conforming to the foregoing provisions on or before February 22, 2006. An application to one financial institution shall satisfy the diligent efforts of this clause.

9. POSSESSION AND CONDITION OF THE PREMISES: Full possession of said premises free of all tenants is to be delivered to the Buyer at the time of delivery of the deed, said premises to be then in the condition as they are now, reasonable wear and tear thereof excepted, and not in violation of local zoning laws. The buyer shall be entitled to an inspection of said premises prior to the delivery of the deed in order to determine whether the condition thereof complies with the terms of this agreement.

10. INSURANCE: The buildings on said premises shall, until the transfer of title hereunder be kept insured in a reasonable amount by the seller and in the event that at the time of transfer of title there is unrestored damage to the said premises from any cause whatsoever, other than reasonable use and wear, in an amount in excess of $5,000 the Buyer shall at his option either take the insurance money or claim, if any, arising out of such damage and fulfill this contract or may cancel this contract and receive back their deposit and in the event such unrestored damage is less than $5,000 Buyer shall take, upon delivery of the deed, the insurance money or claim, if any, and the purchase price will be reduced by the amount of any co-insurance by Seller, uncollectable insurance coverage, and uninsured damage.

11. EXTENSION TO PERFECT TITLE OR MAKE PREMISES CONFORM: If the seller shall be unable to give title or to make conveyance, or to deliver possession of the premises all as herein stipulated, or if at the time of the delivery of

the deed the premises do not conform with the provisions herein, the Seller shall use reasonable efforts to remove any defects in title (which duty to use reasonable efforts to clear title shall not require Seller to spend in excess of $500 except for the payment of mortgages) or to deliver possession as provided herein or to make the said premises conform to the provisions hereof as the case may be, in which event the seller shall give written notice thereof to the Buyer at or before the time for performance hereunder and thereupon the time for performance hereof shall be extended for a period of thirty days. If at the expiration of the extended time the Seller shall have failed so to remove any defects in title, deliver possession, or make the premises conform, as the case may be, all as herein agreed, or if at any time during the period of this Agreement or any extension thereof, the holder of a mortgage on said premises shall refuse to permit the insurance proceeds, if any, to be used for such purposes, then any payments made under this Agreement shall be forthwith refunded and all other obligations of all parties hereto shall cease and this agreement shall be void without recourse to the parties hereof, except that Buyer's right to declare this Agreement void due to damage to the premises prior to the time of delivery of the deed is subject to the rights of the parties as provided in Clause 10 hereof.

12. BUYER'S ELECTION TO ACCEPT TITLE: The Buyer shall have the election, at either the original or any extended time for performance, to accept such title as the Seller can deliver to the said premises in their then condition and to pay therefore the purchase price without deduction, in which case the Seller shall convey such title, except that in the event of such conveyance in accord with the provisions of this clause, if the said premises shall have been damaged by fire, the Seller shall, unless the Seller has previously restored the premises to their former condition, either: a.) Pay over or assign to the buyer on delivery of the deed, all amounts recovered or recoverable on account of such insurance, less any amounts reasonably expended by the Seller for any partial restoration, or b.) if a holder of a mortgage on said premises shall not permit the insurance proceeds or a part thereof to be used to restore the said premises to their former condition or to be so paid over or assigned, Seller shall give to the buyer a credit against the purchase price, on delivery of the deed, equal to said amounts so recovered or recoverable and retained by the holder of the said mortgage less any amounts reasonably expended by the seller for any partial restoration.

13. ACCEPTANCE OF DEED: The acceptance of a deed by the Buyer or his nominee as the case may be, shall be deemed to be a full performance and discharge of every agreement and obligation herein contained or expressed, except such as are by the terms hereof, to be performed after the delivery of said deed.

14. USE OF PURCHASE MONEY TO CLEAR TITLE: To enable the Seller to make conveyance as herein provided, the Seller may, at the time of delivery of the deed, use the purchase money or any portion thereof to clear the title of any or all encumbrances or interests provided that all instruments so procured are recorded simultaneously with the delivery of the deed, or within a reasonable time.

15. ADJUSTMENTS: Collected rents, water rates, sewer use charges, and real estate taxes shall be apportioned as of the day of delivery of the deed. If the amount

of said real estate taxes is not known at the time of the delivery of the deed, they shall be apportioned on the basis of the taxes assessed for the preceding year, with a reapportionment as soon as the new tax rate and valuation can be ascertained; and if the taxes which are to be apportioned shall thereafter be reduced by abatement, the amount of such abatement, less the reasonable cost of obtaining the same, shall be apportioned between the parties, provided that neither party shall be obligated to institute or prosecute proceedings for an abatement unless herein otherwise agreed.

16. BROKERS FEE: There are no brokers in this transaction.

17. BUYER'S DEFAULT: If the buyer shall fail to fulfill his agreements herein all deposits made hereunder by the buyer shall be retained by the seller as liquidated damages, as seller's sole remedy at law or in equity.

18. WARRANTIES: Buyer acknowledges that Buyer had the opportunity to have the premises inspected by persons engaged in the business of conducting home inspections, pest inspections and radon inspections and that in entering into the Agreement, Buyer is not relying upon any warranties or representations made by the Seller, his agents or representatives with regard to the condition of the premises, its structure, siding, roof, electrical, heating, plumbing or other mechanical systems contained therein. Buyer acknowledges that Buyer is buying the premises together with the buildings thereon in their 'as is' condition.

19. CONSTRUCTION OF AGREEMENT: This agreement is to be constructed as a Massachusetts contract, sets forth the entire contract between the parties, and may be canceled, modified or amended only by a written instrument executed by both Buyer and Seller.

20. ADDITIONAL PROVISIONS:
    (a) Seller shall provide smoke detectors as is required by the Massachusetts General Laws and shall prior to transfer deliver to buyer a certificate of compliance by the Fire Department of the City of Boston;
    (b) Buyer has specifically waived the right to a lead paint inspection and assumes all risk that there may be dangerous levels of lead in paint, plasters, soil or other materials on the premises;
    (c) The parties agree to execute any and all usual and customary documents at the time of conveyance including documents customarily required by Buyer's lender;
    (d) Both parties have been informed that they should seek independent legal counsel with respect to this agreement and have done so to their respective satisfactions;
    (e) Buyer and Buyer's agents shall be given reasonable access to the premises subsequent to the execution of this Agreement for the purpose of making required inspections, taking measurements and other related activities. Such access shall be made only with prior notice to the seller.

(f) Seller authorizes the lender's attorney to obtain mortgage payoff figures using the following information:

First Mortgage: Bank   Account #
Second Mortgage: Bank   Account#
Buyer's social security number:

SIGNED AND SEALED ON THE DATE FIRST ABOVE WRITTEN

SELLER: _____

BUYER: _____

RIDER TO PURCHASE AND SALE AGREEMENT

21.   From and after the date of this Agreement, Seller agrees to permit Buyer and its designees, including but not limited to prospective mortgage lenders and insurance agents, reasonable access, at reasonable times, to the said premises and condominium for the purpose of making measurements, inspections and the like. Said right of access shall be exercised only in the presence of Seller and only after reasonable prior notice, either written or oral, to the seller.

22.   Notwithstanding any other provisions of this agreement regarding the conditions of said Unit, at the time of the delivery of the deed hereunder, the unit and all dwelling and daily use areas of the premises shall be broom-swept and clean and free of all Seller's possessions and debris) and shall be delivered free of all building materials such as lumber, insulation, and the like, paints, solvents, chemicals, debris and personal property, and all systems, including but not limited to electrical, plumbing, heating, air conditioning and ventilation systems and all appliances shall be in the same condition at closing as they were on the date of Buyer's inspection, reasonable wear and tear excepted.

23.   The Seller represents that:
   A.   There are no lawsuits pending against or threatened against the Seller, nor to the Seller's best knowledge against the Condominium Trust or Condominium Trust Association.
   B.   There is no pending bankruptcy, mortgage, foreclosure, or other proceeding which might in any material way impact adversely on Seller's ability to perform under this Agreement.
   C.   There are no other rights, e.g. rights of first refusal, or other consents required for of delivery of the deed other than the existing mortgages, if any, on the Premises which Seller shall secure releases for using the purchase money hereunder.
   D.   To the best of Seller's knowledge, there are no underground storage tanks located on the Premises and no articles or substances

on or near the Premises which are toxic or hazardous.

    E.   The Seller has no knowledge of any municipal betterments effecting the Premises voted or contemplated by the city which is likely to result in an assessment against the Premises.

24.   Seller warrants and represents that the Premises are not served by a septic system, but rather, are connected to and served by municipal water and sewer.

25.   Seller will pay buyer a 3% closing cost credit and will pay the Buyer $18,650 for repairs. Both payments will be credited at the closing.

26.   The Seller covets that the first and second floors of the building shall be vacant, and that $1300 will be credited to the Buyer at the closing to cover the monies being held as Last Months' rent for the tenant who currently occupies the third floor. Said tenant shall remain in the building through the closing. Buyer hereby releases and holds Seller harmless for any potential liability relative to the tenant currently occupying the third floor.

27.   Buyer is notified that Seller retains the right to sell the property through a 1031 exchange, and Buyer agrees to cooperate relative to that transaction.

28.   Seller represents that the following are the names, telephone numbers and account numbers of any entity which, as of the date of this agreement, holds a mortgage or other security interest in the premises. This agreement shall constitute Seller's authorization to each entity named below to furnish loan payoff information to Buyer's lender's counsel:

    (i)   Lender:
           Telephone No.:
           Account No.:

    (ii)   Lender:
           Telephone No:
           Account No:

    Buyer: _____

    Seller: _____

Dated:

8. <u>Deed</u>

QUITCLAIM DEED

I, Cristina M. Poulter, aka Cristina Elzeneiny, of 313 Summit Avenue, Unit 5, Brighton, Suffolk County, Massachusetts, for consideration of $248,000, hereby grant to: Svetoslav I. Slavchev and Diana I. Slavchev, presently of 426 Cambridge Street, Cambridge, MA

with Quitclaim Covenants

The unit known as 313 Summit Avenue, Boston (Brighton), MA in the 313-17 Summit Avenue Condominium

a certain parcel of land (952 Morton Street) situated in Dorchester, being shown as Lot No. 2 on a plan made by E.L. Moulton, surveyor, dated April 17, 1919, and recorded with Suffolk Deeds, Book 4476, Page 601, and bounded and described as follows:

NORTHERLY	by Lot No. 1 on said plan (106.04 feet);
SOUTHERLY	by Lot No. 3 on said plan (78.63 feet);
EASTERLY	by land now or late of Julia A. Gallarneauz (45 feet); and
SOUTHWESTERLY	by Morton Street by 2 lines measuring 32.32 feet and 232.34 feet.

Containing 3232 square feet.
For our title, see deed recorded in Book 1817, Page 327.

Signed this___Day of_____, 2008.

Cristina M. Poulter

COMMONWEALTH OF MASSACHUSETTS
SUFFOLK, ss

Then personally appeared the above-named Cristina Poulter who acknowledged the foregoing to be her free act and deed, before me.

Notary Public
My Commission Expires:

9.   Divorce Settlement Agreement

THOMPSON SETTLEMENT AGREEMENT

This Agreement is made this ———— day of ————, 2007 by and between Beth Thompson, presently of 88 Trevor Court, Mission City, Norfolk County, Massachusetts (hereinafter referred to as "Wife") and Sam Thompson, presently of 76 Fleece Boulevard, Mission City, Norfolk County, Massachusetts (hereinafter referred to as "Husband").

WHEREAS the Husband and Wife were married to each other in Sioux City, Montana, on August 7, 1987, and last lived together at Mission City, Norfolk County, Massachusetts, on or about January 1, 2005.

WHEREAS there have been two children born of this marriage: Sam, Jr (DOB 9/4/92) and Cindy (DOB 1/15/98).

WHEREAS Husband and Wife did separate as aforesaid and have lived apart since said date due, <u>inter alia</u>, to the existence of continuing and serious problems between them.

WHEREAS the parties intend to file a Joint Petition for Divorce pursuant to M.G.L. c.208, s.1A in the Norfolk Probate and Family Court.

AND WHEREAS it is the desire and intent, to the extent allowable by applicable law, by this instrument, to provide for and make a complete resolution and settlement of and for all matters relating to the interests and obligations of each with respect to past, present, and future support, property and estate rights, and obligations and liabilities. The foregoing stated purposes are to be interpreted and construed in the most broad and general terms, Husband and Wife intending by this instrument to resolve and determine all rights, interests and obligations arising from and in connection with their marital relationship.

NOW THEREFORE, in consideration of the promises and covenants by and between Husband and Wife herein contained, Husband and Wife do hereby mutually agree as follows:

1. PRIVACY: From the date hereof, Husband and Wife may continue to live separate and apart from one another for the rest of their lives.

2. WAIVER OF RIGHTS OF INHERITANCE: Husband and Wife each hereby waive any right at law or in equity to share in the other's estate in case of intestacy and to elect to take against any last will made by the other, including all rights of dower or of courtesy, and each hereby waives, renounces and relinquishes unto each other, their respective heirs, executors, administrators and assigns forever, all and any interest of any kind or character which either may now have or may hereafter acquire in or to any real or personal property of the other and whether now owned or hereafter acquired by either, except as expressly provided by the terms of this Agreement. Further, Husband and Wife waive the right to act as executor or adminis-

trator, or in any fiduciary capacity whatsoever, under the estate of the other, except to enforce any obligation imposed by this Agreement, or unless otherwise expressly provided for by the terms of this Agreement.

    3.   RELEASE OF CLAIMS: Husband and Wife hereby mutually release and forever discharge each other from any and all actions, suits, debts, claims, demands, and obligations whatsoever, both in law and in equity, which either of them has ever had, now has, or may hereafter have against the other, upon or by reason of any matter, cause or thing up to the date of this Agreement, including, but not limited to, claims against each other's property, it being the intention of the parties that henceforth there shall exist as between them only such rights and obligations as are specifically provided for in this Agreement, in any judgment entered in the parties' divorce action, and as may normally exist between two unrelated natural persons under the laws of the Commonwealth of Massachusetts and the United States.

    4.   NONINCURRENCE OF LIABILITIES BY HUSBAND: Husband warrants, represents and agrees he will not hereafter contract or incur any debt, charge or liability whatsoever for which Wife, her legal representatives, or her property or estate will or may become liable, and that at the time of this Agreement there are no outstanding bills or debts incurred by him which are the obligation of Wife, except as may be hereinafter specified in an Exhibit annexed hereto and initialed by both parties. Husband further covenants at all times to hold Wife free, harmless and indemnified from and against all debts, charges or liabilities previously contracted or incurred by him, or hereafter contracted or incurred by him in breach of the provisions of this paragraph and from any and all reasonable attorney's fees, costs and expenses incurred by Wife as a result of any such breach.

    5.   NONINCURRENCE OF LIABILITIES BY WIFE: Wife warrants, represents and agrees that she will not hereafter contract or incur any debt, charge or liability whatsoever for which Husband, his legal representatives, or his property or estate, will or may become liable, and that at the time of the Agreement there are no outstanding bills incurred by her which are the obligation of the Husband, except as may be hereinafter specified in an Exhibit annexed hereto and initialed by both parties. Wife further covenants at all times to hold Husband free, harmless and indemnified from and against all debts, charges or liabilities previously contracted or incurred by her or hereafter contracted or incurred by her in breach of the provisions of this paragraph, and from any and all reasonable attorney's fees, costs and expenses incurred by Husband as a result of any such breach.

    6.   EXHIBITS: There are annexed hereto and incorporated by reference herein Exhibits I through VIII. Husband and Wife agree to be bound by, and to perform and carry out all the terms of the said Exhibits to the same extent as if each of said Exhibits were fully set forth in the text of this instrument. In such case as there is a conflict with the provisions of any such Exhibit and this Agreement, the provisions of such Exhibit shall control.

    7.   NONVARIANCE OF PROVISIONS: Husband and Wife agree: I) to accept the provisions made for each of them in this Agreement and other undertakings of the other as set forth in this Agreement in full satisfaction and

discharge of all claims, past, present and future, which he or she may have upon the other and which in any way arise out of the marital relationship; 2) to waive any claim to alimony or support for himself or herself, other than as provided in this Agreement; 3) not to seek the entry of an Order of Judgment which differs in any way from the terms of this Agreement; and 4) to indemnify and hold harmless the other from any amount in excess of the actual payments he or she is required to make to the other pursuant to this Agreement.

      8.   ENFORCEMENT OF AGREEMENT: Any breach of any term or terms of this Agreement shall give the non-breaching party the right to take immediate action, either at law or in equity, concerning such breach. If either Husband or Wife shall commit a breach of any of the provisions of this Agreement and legal action required to enforce such provisions shall be instituted by the other, the prevailing party shall be entitled to reasonable attorneys' fees and costs as determined by the Court. No forbearance and/or failure by a party hereto to seek enforcement upon a breach of any term or terms hereof, or to insist upon strict compliance herewith, shall constitute a waiver of such term or terms or such party's right upon a subsequent breach to seek enforcement of any term or terms hereof.

      9.   PARTIAL INVALIDITY: In the event that any part of this Agreement shall be held invalid, such invalidity shall not invalidate the whole Agreement, but the remaining provisions of this Agreement shall continue to be valid and binding to the extent that such provisions continue to reflect fairly the intent and understanding of the parties.

      10.   CONSTRUCTION: This Agreement shall be construed and governed according to the Laws of the Commonwealth of Massachusetts and shall survive the death of the Husband or the death of the Wife, binding their heirs, estates and assigns, provided, however, that to the extent that a party's life insurance or other death benefit fulfills his or her obligations under this Agreement, no claim shall accrue against the heirs, estate or assigns of the deceased party.

      11.   HEADINGS: Headings and paragraph numbering as used in this Agreement are for convenience only and shall not affect the meaning or construction hereof.

      12.   ENTIRE UNDERSTANDING: The parties have incorporated their entire understanding in this Agreement. Neither party is relying on any promises or warranties other than those expressly contained in this Agreement. In negotiating and executing this Agreement, each party has relied on the other's Rule 401 Financial Statement which each affirms fully and accurately discloses all assets, liabilities, income and expenses. Furthermore, each party warrants and represents that he or she has disclosed all assets held by another for his or her benefit. Each party acknowledges that he or she has had the opportunity to obtain discovery from the other and waives the right to further discovery in connection with this divorce action.

      13.   EQUITABLE DIVISION: The parties hereto enter into this Agreement acknowledging that, pursuant to Massachusetts General Laws, Chapter 208, s.34, as amended, they may each have rights in the other's assets; that they have been fully informed of same by their counsel and of the criteria set forth in Massachu-

setts General Laws, Chapter 208, s.34, upon which said rights would be determined; that they are each aware of said rights and criteria; that they have each fully disclosed to each other all their respective assets; and that they have made an equitable division of their assets in this Agreement in accordance with the provisions of Chapter 208, s.34. The Husband and Wife each accept the covenants of the other in complete satisfaction of said rights. Therefore, except as set forth herein, in consideration of the mutual covenants of the parties contained herein, the Husband and the Wife each hereby waive all claims and rights they may have against the other party for support of any kind, separate maintenance or alimony and further waive all claims and rights they may have under Massachusetts General Laws, Chapter 208, s.34, as amended.

Upon the execution of the within Agreement, except as otherwise set forth herein, the Husband's and the Wife's obligations to the other for alimony, support, transfer, conveyance, gift, assignment or other obligations under Chapter 208, s.34 shall cease, and the Husband and Wife shall forever be discharged with respect thereto.

14. VOLUNTARINESS: Husband and Wife acknowledge and affirm that each of them has entered into this Agreement freely and voluntarily, after full and complete disclosure, contemplation and understanding of its terms and conditions; that each has done so without any interference, undue influence, coercion or fraud by one as to the other; and that accordingly, they do mutually assent and agree to each and every item, and the particulars thereof, contained herein.

15. PRESENTATION TO COURT: At any hearing upon the parties' Joint Petition for Divorce, a copy of this Agreement shall be submitted to the Court and shall be incorporated but not merged in the Judgment of Divorce, and shall survive the same and be thereafter forever binding upon Husband and Wife, their heirs, estates and assigns, excepting that the provisions relating to the children as set forth in the Exhibits attached hereto shall merge. The purposes of this paragraph are: 1) to protect both parties against any attempt by the other party to vary the terms of this Agreement after the entry of a final judgment; 2) to enable Husband and Wife to procure an enforcement of the terms of this Agreement incorporated in a Judgment of Divorce in the Probate Court or as to a binding contract in any Court with jurisdiction over the person or property of the other party; and 3) to protect the welfare and best interests of the children.

16. DOCUMENTS: Whenever called upon to do so by the other party, each party shall forthwith execute, acknowledge and deliver to or for the other party without consideration any and all deeds, assignments, bills of sale or other instruments that may be necessary or convenient to carry out the provisions of this Agreement, or that may be required to enable the other party to sell, encumber, hypothecate or otherwise dispose of the property now or hereafter owned or acquired by such other party.

EXHIBIT I

Waiver of Alimony

A. In consideration of the payments, mutual covenants, conditions and promises made herein, and in consideration of all relevant facts and circumstances, including but not limited to the financial circumstances of the respective parties and employment of both, each party does hereby release the other from any and all claims for past, present and future alimony, separate support or any other payments whatever on account of their marriage to one another.

EXHIBIT II

Custody and Parenting Schedule
Child Support and College

A. The parties shall have shared legal custody of the children, and the Wife shall have physical custody.

B. <u>Parenting Schedule:</u>
 1. The children shall be with the Husband every other weekend from Friday after school until Monday morning when he shall take them to school.
 2. The children shall have dinner with the Husband on Tuesdays and Thursdays from 6:00 P.M. to 7:30 P.M.
 3. The parties agree to work together to maintain a workable schedule and to be flexible if and when it is necessary for the children's best interest.

C. <u>Holidays and Vacations:</u> The parties agree to share time with the children on major holidays and school vacations. Specifically:
 1. The parties shall alternate having the children for February and April school vacations, and shall divide Christmas vacation equally.
 2. Each parent may spend at least two weeks vacation with the children during the summer (which shall accommodate their summer activities). The vacationing parent may remove the children from the Commonwealth of Massachusetts for such vacations, provided that the vacationing party shall provide the other party with reasonable notice of his or her vacations plans in advance, and a telephone number and address where he or she may be reached; and provided further that neither

party shall take the children out of the country without the written consent of the other parent, which consent shall not be unreasonably withheld or delayed.

3. Monday holidays shall be with the parent who has the children over the preceding weekend.

4. Secular and religious holidays and the children's birthdays may be shared or alternated, as the parties may agree.

5. The Husband and Wife shall accommodate each other to allow the children to spend Father's Day, Mother's Day, the parties' birthdays and other significant life events with the appropriate parent.

6. Each parent shall be solely responsible for the cost of day care or child care, if any, during any vacation period or portion thereof when the children are or scheduled to be with him or her.

D. Each parent shall encourage love, affection and respect for the other parent in their children, and neither parent shall attempt or condone any attempt to estrange the children from the other parent or to injure or impede the children's respect or affection for the other parent.

E. Both parties shall confer with each other in good faith to reach all major decisions (including but not limited to educational, medical, religious, and financial) affecting children. Only in an emergency situation shall any such decision be made without the agreement of both parties. In such event, either party shall make the decision and immediately notify the other party.

F. Commencing May 2, 2007, the Husband shall pay the Wife the sum of One Thousand Dollars per month on the first day of each month by electronic transfer to the Wife's bank account of which $900 shall be designated as child support and $100 as 50% of the family's health and dental insurance. The parties intend that the child support payments described herein shall cover the children's ordinary, day-to-day expenses such as food, clothing and the like as well as the Husband's 50% share of the family health insurance premium. In addition, the Wife shall notify the Husband in writing in a timely manner if there is any increase or decrease in the cost of the family's medical and/or dental insurance premiums, and the Husband's support obligation shall be adjusted accordingly.

G. <u>Extraordinary expenses</u>: The parties agree that they will share extraordinary expenses for the children, including but not limited to counseling, orthodontia, and camp and summer programs on a 50/50 basis. Neither party shall incur any extraordinary expense without the consent of the other, which consent shall not be unreasonably withheld or delayed. Commencing March 1, 2006, the Husband shall also contribute 25% of the children's educational costs to be capped at $5,500.00 per year ($460.00 per month) toward the costs of the children's pre-school and private day school.

H. At the time of the second child's emancipation as defined below, the parties' obligations as defined herein shall terminate. A child shall be deemed emancipated for all purposes of this Agreement on the first to occur of the following:

1. Attaining the age of 18 or three months after graduation from high school, whichever occurs later, unless a child is domiciled with a parent and is principally dependent upon him or her for maintenance in which case any obligation shall continue until the time the child reaches the age of 21, unless the child has been accepted to college or a vocational training school as a full time student (in which case subparagraph 2 below shall apply);
2. If a child is attending a post-secondary accredited vocational training school or college as a full-time student, at age 23 or the completion of an undergraduate college degree or its equivalent, whichever occurs first. If a child is emancipated on account of leaving college or delaying his or her entrance into college after high school graduation, and then re-enrolls or enters college before age 23, he or she shall be deemed unemancipated upon resumption of his education until the occurrence of another emancipating event;
3. Marriage;
4. Permanent residence away from the residence of both parties. Residence at boarding school, camp or college is not to be deemed emancipation;
5. Death;
6. Entry into the military service of the United States; and
7. Engaging in full-time employment after the age of 18, except that full-time employment during vacation and summer periods shall not be deemed emancipation.

I. <u>College.</u> The parties agree that the choice of college for the children shall be made with due regard for their aptitudes, interests and desires, and after consideration of the attendant expenses. They further agree that the children should receive the best college educations available to them. The parties agree to share the costs of college taking into consideration their respective incomes, assets and liabilities. Any agreement between the parties regarding the choice of college and allocation of costs shall be in writing. In the event the parties cannot agree on the choice of college or allocation of college expenses, they agree to submit the matter to mediation and if mediation is unsuccessful, then either party may seek judicial resolution of the issue. The cost of mediation shall be shared equally by the parties unless the mediator allocates the cost differently. Costs of college education shall include admission and placement examination fees, admission application fees, reasonable pre-admission college-visit expenses, tuition, board and room, books, laboratory and other fees customarily included on the institution's tuition bill, and normal transportation expenses in traveling to and from the college or university at term breaks and vacation periods. It is expected that the children will contribute to the degree they are able to do so to their college educations through their own funds, scholarship or other donative aid, summer earnings, student loans and other forms of financial aid.

EXHIBIT III

Division of Marital Assets

A. Husband and Wife agree to divide the assets of the marriage so as to achieve an equitable division thereof pursuant to M.G.L. c. 208, s.34 as follows:

 1. <u>Real Estate</u>: The marital residence located at 20 Burger Place, Finster, Massachusetts, has been sold. Simulta neously with the execution of this Agreement, the Wife shall receive the sum of $22,520.00 as her share of the net proceeds of the sale, and the Husband shall retain the remainder of said proceeds.

 2. <u>Personalty:</u> The parties have arrived at an equitable and mutually satisfactory division of all personal property, bank accounts, and investment accounts. Simultaneously with the execution of this Agreement, the Husband shall transfer title of the 1979 Rolls Royce to the Wife who shall assume sole responsi bility for the car loan and car insurance on said vehicle.

 3. The parties agree that the Husband will transfer 50% of his shares in Alcoa stock to the Wife within thirty (30) days of the date of Court approval of this Agreement, or if such transfer is not possible because of corporate restrictions, then the Husband agrees to hold 50% of said stock in trust for the Wife's benefit.

 4. <u>Retirement and Pension Plans</u>: Each party shall be entitled to retain his or her interest in any pension plan, IRA, profit-sharing plan, annuity or other retirement account or plan in his or her own name; each waives any interest in such pension or retirement plans of other; and, upon request, each agrees to execute all documents necessary to permit the other party to change beneficia ries of any such pension or retirement plans.

B. The parties agree to execute all documents necessary to accomplish the terms of this Agreement, including but not limited to changes in pension or life insurance beneficiaries, whenever such documents are presented for signature.

C. Husband and Wife agree that their retention of their individually owned assets and the transfers and releases herein before provided in this Exhibit accomplish and represent a fair and equitable division of all marital property pursuant to Massachusetts General Laws, Chapter 208, s.34. Each shall have sole and exclusive ownership of the property retained or acquired hereunder, free of all claims of the other party.

D. Nothing in this Agreement and/or Exhibits shall in any manner or form interfere and/or affect either party's ownership or interest in and/or to any property of whatever kind or nature not herein provided for, nor transferred hereunder, nor hereafter acquired, and therefore, all such property, whether in either's name individually or with another party or which they may have any interest in whatsoever, now or hereafter, shall be the sole property of such party, free from any claim by the other.

EXHIBIT IV

Marital Debts

A. Husband and Wife acknowledge and affirm that, save for debts of a personal nature, which are and shall remain their separate responsibility, and/or debts solely the responsibility of each, there are no marital debts.

B. The Husband and Wife shall each be responsible for their own legal fees related to negotiating this Agreement and obtaining a divorce.

C. Husband and Wife covenant and agree that neither of them shall use any heretofore joint credit cards or charge or bank accounts, and shall be fully responsible for payment of their own bills.

EXHIBIT V

Medical Insurance and Medical Expenses

A. The Wife covenants and agrees that she will maintain and pay for medical insurance coverage comparable to existing coverage for the children under her family plan medical insurance policies until such time as the second child is emancipated or no longer eligible for such coverage. During any period when a child is covered by the Wife's family medical insurance plan, the parties acknowledge and agree that the Husband shall also be covered at no additional cost to either party. At such time as the second child is emancipated or is no longer eligible for coverage under the Wife's policy, the Wife agrees to maintain medical insurance coverage comparable to existing coverage for the Husband until such time as he no longer wishes such coverage or remarries or is no longer eligible for such coverage or as of the death of either party, provided, however, that the Husband shall reimburse the Wife for any additional cost of such insurance attributable solely to his coverage under the policy, i.e. the difference between a plan covering the Wife individually and a plan covering both Husband and Wife.

B. Pursuant to M.G.L. c.175, s.110(I), or another analogous continuation coverage statute, remarriage by the Wife shall in no manner or form affect her obligations under Paragraph A of this Exhibit. If the Wife remarries, and law then existing permits maintenance of medical insurance coverage for the Husband as now exists pursuant to M.G.L. c. 175, s.110 (I) (b) or another analogous continuation coverage statute, the Husband may choose to be covered by the Wife's plan, provided that he shall reimburse her for any extra cost for such coverage.C. In the event the Wife is unable to work, or is unable to obtain medical insurance coverage through her employment, the parties agree that the Husband shall obtain and pay for such insurance coverage comparable to existing coverage for the children under a family medical insurance policy until such time as the second child is emancipated or is no longer eligible for such coverage. During any period when the children are covered by the Husband's family health insurance plan, the parties acknowledge and agree that the Wife shall also be covered at no additional cost to either party. Under the circumstances described in this Paragraph C, the Husband agrees to maintain insurance coverage comparable to existing coverage for the Wife until such time as she no longer wishes such coverage or remarries or is no longer eligible for such coverage or as of the death of either party, provided, however, if the Wife chooses to remain on the Husband's medical insurance plan after the emancipation of the second child, she shall reimburse the Husband for any additional cost of such insurance attributable solely to her coverage under the policy, i.e. the difference between a plan covering the Husband individually and a plan covering both Husband and Wife. Pursuant to M.G.L. c.175, s.110(I), or another analogous continuation coverage statute, remarriage by the Husband shall in no manner or form affect his obligations under Paragraph C of this Exhibit. If the Husband remarries, and law then existing permits maintenance of health insurance coverage for the Wife as now exists pursuant to M.G.L. c.175, s.110(I)(b) or another analogous continuation coverage statute, the Wife may choose to be covered by the Husband's plan, provided that she shall reimburse him for any extra cost for such coverage.

   C. In the event that the Wife, through no fault or action of the Husband, becomes ineligible for coverage under the Husband's medical insurance plan as described in Paragraph C above, or if the Wife chooses to obtain medical insurance for herself on an individual plan, she agrees to provide and pay for her own health insurance coverage.

   D. In the event that the Husband, through no fault or action of the Wife, becomes ineligible for coverage under the Wife's medical insurance plan as described in Paragraph A above, the Husband agrees to provide and pay for such insurance coverage for himself.

<u>EXHIBIT VI</u>

<u>Life Insurance</u>

   A. In order to fulfill their obligations under this Agreement, the Husband and Wife agree to maintain life insurance coverage on their respective lives in the amount of at least One Million ($1,000,000.00) Dollars in trust for the benefit of the children.

B.   The parties further agree that they will not permit said insurance to lapse or expire and that they will not surrender, sell, assign, pledge or any other manner divest themselves of control of the policies except with the written consent of the other. They further agrees not to borrow against any cash value of said life insurance policies. If, on the death of either party, it is found that any of his or her policy or policies have lapsed so that the aggregate insurance coverage is less than the minimum obligation under this Exhibit, the surviving party, on behalf of the children, shall be entitled to make a preferred creditor's claim against the deceased party's estate for the face value of any such lapsed policy to the extent necessary to fulfill any and all obligations under this Exhibit.

C.   Whenever reasonably requested by the either party, but no more frequently than once a year, the other party shall furnish to him or her satisfactory evidence that said life insurance policies or equivalent death benefits are in full force and effect.

D.   Remarriage by either party or additional children born to either party shall in no manner or form affect his or her obligations under this Exhibit.

E.   Simultaneously with the execution of this Agreement, the Husband shall transfer ownership of the Wife's life insurance policy to the Wife, and thereafter, the Wife shall assume sole responsibility for paying the premiums on said policy and any additional policy she may obtain.

Husband: _____

Wife: _____

10. Motion for Temporary Orders

COMMONWEALTH OF MASSACHUSETTS
MIDDLESEX, ss
                              Probate & Family Court
                              Docket No. 05D3987

Max Martin, *plaintiff*	)))
v.	))
Sally Martin, *Defendant*	)) } }

Plaintiff's Emergency Motion for Temporary Orders

Now comes the Plaintiff and hereby moves this court to issue the following temporary orders: 1) joint physical custody; 2) joint legal custody; and 3) for reasonable visitation for the Plaintiff to include overnight visits in Cambridge, MA. As grounds in support, he submits his Affidavit (Exhibit 'A') and states:

1. The parties were married on May 3, 2002 in Raleigh, North Carolina and established domicile in Cambridge, Massachusetts in February 2003;
2. The Plaintiff is employed as a janitor;
3. The parties' two children, Timmie (age 5) and Tommy (age 6) are staying in Raleigh, North Carolina with the defendant and her parents and are enrolled in the public school system in that jurisdiction;
4. The boys are involved in many community activities and have established friendships in the Cambridge area, having lived there for the majority of their lives;
5. The Plaintiff has assumed an active and primary role in raising the boys since their respective births. His work allows for long periods of time-off and flexible hours, permitting his heightened involvement in their lives;
6. The Defendant has opted to remain in Raleigh with her parents, thus abandoning the boys;
7. The Defendant has denied reasonable visitation to the plaintiff, specifically overnights in Cambridge. The Defendant's relationship with the boys, not to mention their 'best interests', has been compromised as a result.

8. On June 14, 2007, this Court (Winnington, J.) vacated its prior order awarding physical custody to the plaintiff. Following the hearing (enclosed as Exhibit 'C'), counsel forwarded the reference to an on-point case (Jack v. Jill, Docket No. 06-P-080, a Massachusetts Appellate Decision on appeal from the Barnstable Probate & Family Court in August 2006) to the Court. Said case spoke to the probative value of deception insofar as it resulted in children residing in a foreign jurisdiction more than 6 months. It mirrors the facts in this case, clearly supporting the plaintiff's contentions. This Court did not consider said case.

WHEREFORE, the Plaintiff requests this Honorable Court enter an order for joint physical custody, joint legal custody, and substantial visitation for the plaintiff to include overnights in Cambridge.

Respectfully submitted,
PLAINTIFF
By his attorney,

_____

Jeremy T. Robin
15 Court Square
Boston, MA 02108
(617) 227-0838
BBO #629107

CERTIFICATE OF SERVICE

I, Jeremy T. Robin, attorney for the Plaintiff, do hereby certify that on this day I served a copy of this document by mail to the Defendant's Attorney:

Jack Leeman, Esq.
12 East Avenue
Plainville, MA 02144

_____

Jeremy T. Robin

Dated:

11.   Personal Injury Demand Letter

September 26, 2007

Mary Hack
Claims Department
Safety Insurance Co.
20 Custom House Street
Boston, MA 02110

RE:
    Your Insured: Charles Chacks
    Our Claimant: Holly Chacks (minor)
    Your Claim#:   12345
    Date Of Loss: 11/2/06

Dear Ms. Hack:

As you are aware, this office represents Holly Anna Chacks, relative to injuries she sustained due to the negligence of your insured.

Following is a summary of and written offer to compromise and settle Miss Chack's claim. This letter and the accompanying materials are submitted solely for the purpose of exploring settlement. Miss Chack reserves the right to assert and prove additional facts, liability, and damages should this matter fail to resolve prior to litigation. As this letter and the accompanying materials are submitted for the purpose of compromising a dispute, they should not be construed as admissible nor discoverable evidence should litigation of this matter become necessary.

FACTS

On or about November 2, 2006, Miss Chacks was the restrained front seat passenger of a Hundai Accent motor vehicle owned and operated by your insured. Your insured was traveling on Route 3 in Dorchester, MA and struck the vehicle in front of it. Miss Chacks experienced sharp pain in her neck, upper back, right leg and low back.She received chiropractic treatment at Siskal Spine Center, consisting of chiropractic manipulation, intersegmental traction, and heat therapy. She continued to complain of knee pain, so she was referred to the Boston Medical Center for x-rays. Views of her knee and ankle showed slight fractures.

LIABILITY

By striking the vehicle in front of it, your insured committed negligent acts. Those negligent acts proximately caused Miss Chack's injuries, who was a passenger in your insured's vehicle.

INJURIES

Miss Chack sustained the following injuries as a result of this accident:
1. Acute traumatic cervical sprain/strain associated with intersegmental joint dysfunction 847.0;
2. Acute traumatic cervical sprain/strain associated with intersegmental joint dysfunction 847.1
3. Acute traumatic cervical sprain/strain associated with intersegmental joint dysfunction 847.2
4. Slight knee fracture;
5. Slight ankle fracture.

MEDICAL EXPENSES

Miss Chack incurred the following medical expenses as a result of his injuries:

Siskal Spine Center
$2000

Boston Medical Center
$1000

TOTAL $3000

DEMAND

In light of the significant physical pain and suffering, lengthy period of disability, trauma, knee and ankle fractures, caused by the negligence and intentional conduct of your insured, added difficulty completing daily tasks and the inability to live her life in a normal manner (18 weeks of partial disability), all endured by Miss Chack as a result of this accident, this office demands **$9500** as full and final settlement of this matter.

Kindly contact me after reviewing your file.

Very truly yours,

Jeremy T. Robin

12.   Hourly Fee Agreement

ATTORNEY/CLIENT HOURLY FEE AGREEMENT

The LAW OFFICES OF JEREMY T. ROBIN ("Attorney") agrees to represent Polly McDermott Client") relative to the following matter: Probate Court case for custody/visitation. A retainer of $5000 is required to commence work, at the reduced rate of $225/hr. Any monies unearned at the conclusion of the matter will be refunded, and once retainer is exhausted an additional retainer will be required or attorney will withdraw as counsel.

All legal work (e.g. document drafting, communications, meetings, court hearings, etc.) relative to the representation shall be billed in quarter hour increments. If the legal fees retainer is exhausted prior to completion of legal services, an additional retainer will be due. Failure to promptly pay when a retainer is exhausted will represent a breach of this agreement and will permit Attorney the ability to withdraw from representation.

By signing this agreement, Client understands that Attorney does not and cannot guarantee a certain result. In that regard, Attorney only promises he will use his best efforts to achieve a favorable resolution. By signing, client promises to be respectful and courteous at all times. Attorney covets to provide reasonable updates on the status of the case. Excessive phone calls by clients may require Attorney's withdrawal.

We believe that fees should be openly discussed by lawyer and client. If there are any questions about your bills or fee arrangements, please feel free to call our office. We look forward to vigorously serving you.

_____   _____
Polly McDermott   Jeremy T. Robin

Dated: 8/28/07

13.   Flat Fee Agreement

ATTORNEY/CLIENT FLAT FEE AGREEMENT

The LAW OFFICES OF JEREMY T. ROBIN ("Attorney") agrees to represent Ed Brinstone ("Client") for a flat legal fee of $1500 ($500 received today, $1000 due 8/29/07), relative to the following: filing an appearance in the contempt case in Suffolk Probate Court, moving to change the hearing date, all work up to and including the rescheduled hearing. Should additional work become necessary (e.g. any additional hearings) an additional fee will be required.

We believe that fees should be openly discussed by lawyer and client. If there are any questions about your bills or fee arrangements, please feel free to call our office. We look forward to vigorously serving you.

_____   _____

Edward Brinstone   Jeremy T. Robin

Dated: 8/23/08

14.   Contingent Fee Agreement

CONTINGENT FEE AGREEMENT

The client, Jane Jimmons, retains Attorney Jeremy T. Robin ("the Attorney") to perform the legal services described in Paragraph 1 below. The Attorney agrees to perform them faithfully and with due diligence.

(1)   The claim, controversy, and other matters with reference to which the services are to be performed are: auto accident on Nov 14 '06.

(2)   The contingency upon which compensation is to be paid is the recovery (by verdict, compromise, settlement or otherwise) of money, property of any description or any other thing of value.

(3)   Reasonable compensation on the foregoing contingency is to be paid by the client to the attorney, but such compensation (including that of any associated counsel) is <u>1/3 of gross recovery</u>.

(4)   The client is, in any event, to be liable to the attorney for reasonable expenses and disbursements, including but not limited to all expenses in the engaging of investigators and expert witnesses, delivery charges, deposition expenses (including transcript costs and court reporters' fees, court costs, witness fees, etc.).

(5)   If the attorney is discharged by the client prior to the conclusion of this representation, the attorney is entitled to be then compensated for his reasonable expenses and disbursements. If a lawsuit has been filed prior to discharge, the attorney has an automatic lien as to his fee, pursuant to Massachusetts law.

I HAVE READ THE ABOVE AGREEMENT BEFORE SIGNING IT:

_____

Jane Jimmons

_____

Attorney Jeremy Robin

Dated: 7/25/07

AFTERWARD

Self-determination has been the largest contributor to my happiness. How great it feels to take control of your destiny! For me, regardless of the result, I draw comfort, satisfaction and knowledge by performing a task on my own. My self-esteem expands. In contrast, when I call on others, especially self-acclaimed 'experts', feelings of inadequacy surface. Moreover, these experts often perform at a sub-standard level and have less regard for quality than I do.

As you press forward in self-advocacy, quarantine your personal demons and the unsupportive opinions of others. Then you are half-way home.

With persistence as your partner and justice as your guide, I wish you good luck and Godspeed!